THE ENCYCLOPEDIA OF
DECORATIVE
PAINT
EFFECTS

THE ENCYCLOPEDIA OF
DECORATIVE
PAINT
EFFECTS

A unique A-Z directory of decorative paint effects, plus guidance on how to use them

SIMON CAVELLE

HEADLINE

A QUARTO BOOK

Copyright © 1994 Quarto Publishing plc
First published in Great Britain in 1994 by
HEADLINE BOOK PUBLISHING

First published in softback in 1996
by HEADLINE BOOK PUBLISHING

Reprinted 1997, 1998

All rights reserved. No part of this publication may be
reproduced, stored in a retrieval system, or transmitted, in any
form or by any means, without the prior permission in writing
of the publisher, nor be otherwise circulated in any form of
binding or cover other than that in which it is published and
without a similar condition being imposed on the
subsequent purchaser.

HEADLINE BOOK PUBLISHING
A division of Hodder Headline PLC
338 Euston Road
London NW1 3BH

British Library Cataloguing in Publication Data

Cavelle, Simon
Encyclopedia of Decorative Paint Effects
1. Title
745.7

ISBN 0-7472-7801-6

This book was designed and produced by
Quarto Publishing plc
The Old Brewery
6 Blundell Street
London N7 9BH

Senior editor Sally MacEachern
Copy editor Mary Senechal
Senior art editor Penny Cobb
Designers Clare Baggaley, Karen Skänberg
Photographers Chas Wilder, John Wyland
Picture researchers Dipika Parmar-Jenkins and Anna Kobryn
Picture manager Rebecca Horsewood
Art director Moira Clinch
Publishing director Janet Slingsby

Typeset by Genesis Typesetting, Laser Quay, Rochester, Kent
Manufactured in Singapore by Colour Trend, Singapore
Printed in Singapore by Star Standard Industries (Pte) Ltd

PUBLISHER'S NOTE

Working with paints,
mediums and varnishes
demands care, as some of
the mineral pigments used
in paints are poisonous,
and the solvents are highly
toxic. Always follow the
manufacturer's instructions
regarding safety, and store
chemicals and other toxic
substances well out of
reach of children. Neither
the author, copyright holder
nor publisher can accept
any liability for accidents.

Introduction

Many people admire decorative paint effects, such as false marbling or woodgraining, but feel they could never achieve them without employing the assistance of a professional. Professional paint effect experts are often secretive and do everything in their power to maintain an air of mystery and secrecy. In truth, however, anyone, with a little practice and determination, can produce pleasing and successful results.

This book is written with the aim of making a range of paint effects accessible to everyone, from the more experienced decorator to the complete amateur who has never used a paintbrush before. If you are a beginner you will probably find techniques such as sponging easier than some of the more specialist effects such as gilding or *trompe l'oeil*, but don't be afraid to be adventurous. All the techniques described can be tackled by the amateur, provided you read the instructions carefully.

The modern decorator has access to a huge range of colours and textures. While it's true that decorative effects are more challenging than just applying a simple coat of gloss or emulsion, they are also more fun to do. And the results can transform a quite ordinary room into a very special and individual environment. So, be brave: the first step is always the most difficult but, once it's made, there will be no looking back.

SIMON CAVELLE

Contents

5
Introduction

8
Colour

10
Paints, mediums and varnishes

17
Preparation

22
Equipment

29
Finishing

32
Decorative effects

34
Antiquing

46
Check rolling

47
Colour washing

49
Combing

54
Dragging

57
Faux bamboo

59
Faux stone blocks

62
Flogging

63
Graining

69
Lapis lazuli

71
Liming

73
Malachite

75
Marbling

84 Pickling

86 Porphyry

88 Ragging

94 Sandstone and lichen

96 Spattering

98 Sponging

104 Stippling

109 Sugi

111 Tortoiseshell

116 Verdigris

118 Artistic effects

120 Découpage

122 Gilding

128 Stencilling

136 Trompe l'oeil

138 Themes

140 Floors

143 Walls

152 Furniture

165 Decorated accessories

172 Index

175 Credits

Colour

Understanding colour

Colour mixing depends a great deal on getting to know the individual hues and how they react with one another. The colour circle is a way of showing colours' foremost characteristics.

At the centre of the circle are the primary colours: red, yellow and blue. These are the three truly pure colours from which all other colours are derived. The secondary colours are those produced by mixing each primary colour with its neighbour: red and yellow make orange, yellow and blue make green, blue and red make purple. In other words, these are the second generation of colours.

The next generation, mixed from two secondaries, are called tertiary colours, and the same exercise of mixing adjacent colours to produce different hues can continue until a full spectrum is produced.

Complementary colours
Complementary colours are those that lie directly opposite each other in the colour circle. Because they are opposite they react strongly with each other. Yellow and violet, for example, when placed side by side, become more vibrant, and in some cases seem to flicker. Such effects have long been used not only by leading artists, but for commercial purposes too. Oranges and tangerines are often wrapped in purple tissue paper. Butchers display their meat decorated with plastic greenery.

When complementary colours are mixed, they produce a mid-tone, or grey. Because they are so strongly opposed, they become unbiased – rather as mixing a strong acid with a strong alkaline produces a neutral. This effect can be very useful in colour mixing. If a colour is too vibrant, the tendency might be to add black. However, this action would dirty the colour. If the complementary colour is added, a less vibrant but still clean colour will result.

The colour circle can also be divided into warm and

Understanding colour

◆

Using colour

PRIMARIES

Cold red

Warm red

Warm blue

Warm yellow

Cold blue

Cold yellow

SECONDARIES

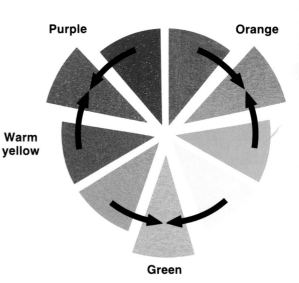

Purple

Orange

Green

cold colours: blues and greens being cold, reds and yellows being warm. Remember, however, that the colours in the circle are pure colours and owe their qualities to their position in the spectrum. Blues can be warm (with the addition of yellow, for example), and reds may be cold.

A tint is made by adding white to a pure colour, reducing its strength and increasing its opacity. A shade comes from adding black to a colour, which reduces its vividness and darkens it. A large amount of coloured paint sold today is either a tint or a shade. However, care should be taken when mixing tints and shades, as they can easily become muddy.

COMPLEMENTARIES

Yellow

Mixture

Purple

Mixture

Green

Red

Using colour

Before deciding on your colour scheme and selecting a decorative paint effect, think about the room you are decorating. Is it naturally light or dark? Is it to be used throughout the day, or just in the evening – as a dining-room, for example? Is the finish more or less important than the colour? The answers to these questions will help you make your decision.

You can visually alter the dimensions of a room by your choice of colour. Warm colours, used strongly, appear to advance and reduce the size of a room, while cool colours seem to recede and give an impression of space. Diagrams 1 and 2 help to illustrate this point. Each features an identical room, one with the back wall painted in a warm colour and one in a cool colour. The coloured ceiling in diagram 3 reduces the height of the room, as does painting the ceiling and upper walls (diagram 4). Lighter colours above darker ones as in diagrams 5 and 6, help to give an impression of space and height.

COLOUR AND SPACE

1 Warm advances

2 Cool recedes

3 Ceiling only painted

4 Ceiling and upper wall painted to picture rail

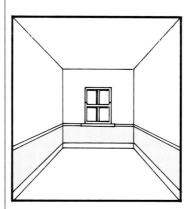

5 Walls painted below dado

6 Walls only painted

Paints, Mediums and Varnishes

Glazes

◆

Mixing colours

◆

Applied and subtractive finishes

◆

Applying paints

There is a bewildering range of paints, mediums and varnishes available. This book is not primarily concerned with standard emulsion, eggshell and gloss paints, but focuses on the paints, mediums and varnishes used to achieve decorative paint effects. The chart opposite lists the main types, with their uses, solvents, advantages and disadvantages.

A medium is a liquid in which pigment is suspended. Although paints in general can be described as mediums, in the context of this book a medium is a glaze or a wash. The two types of medium addressed are water-based and oil-based. Oil mediums dry more slowly and are more durable than water-based mediums. This can be an advantage if the finish is to be worked while wet, or is expected to suffer wear and tear. However, while it is wet, it remains vulnerable. The most awkward aspect of the oil-based mediums, however, is their tendency to yellow.

Name	Solvent
Artists' powder paint	Water
Universal stainers	White spirit
Artists' oil colours	White spirit
Gouache colours	Water
Undercoat	White spirit
Eggshell	White spirit
Gloss	White spirit
Matt emulsion	Water
Silk or satin emulsion	Water
Gloss emulsion	Water
Artists' acrylic colours	Water
Transparent oil glaze	White spirit
Emulsion glaze	Water
Oil-based primer	White spirit
Nitro-cellulose spray or acrylic lacquers	Benzol/acetone
Polyurethane varnish	White spirit
Japan gold-size varnish	White spirit
Shellac (French enamel varnish)	Methylated spirit

PAINTS, MEDIUMS AND VARNISHES

Uses	Advantages	Disadvantages
For tinting oil- or water-based mediums.	Lovely vivid colours which can be used with any medium.	Quite difficult to dissolve, usually leaving some particles at the base of the container that need to be strained off. Normally needs sealer or varnish.
Very strong stainers used by decorators to tint paints and glazes.	Called universal because they can tint oil- or water-based mediums, are cheap for the amount of tinting they offer, and easy to mix.	Limited range of colours and may react badly with some oil glazes.
Tints for oil-based paint, glazes or varnishes.	High-quality colours. Can be thinned with oil or spirit.	Some colours can be extremely expensive. Very slow drying.
For painting designs onto a surface or tinting water-based paints and glazes.	Exceptionally strong colours and therefore good for tinting.	Very expensive. Can only be used with water-based paints and glazes.
Gives a solid colour in preparation for gloss or eggshell.	Easy to apply and dries in 8 to 12 hours. Widely available. Pleasant matt finish.	Not a finish in itself, and requires further coats of gloss, eggshell or varnish.
Top coat for walls and wood. Can be oil-based for a slight sheen, or water-based for a fast-drying finish.	Good colour range. Ideal finish as a ground for paint effects. Wears well – less than gloss but longer than matt emulsion.	Costs more and takes longer to dry than undercoat. Can sometimes be too transparent and need an extra coat.
Oil-based top coat for woodwork.	Smart, hard-wearing and resistant to dirt. Readily available in extensive colour ranges.	Takes longer to dry than other paints. Any flaws will be more apparent due to the shiny surface.
Most time-efficient and cost-effective way of decorating a wall. Water-based, in a wide range of pale colours. Can be diluted for washes.	Quick to apply and fast-drying – recoatable in four hours. Very little smell. Does not show imperfections. Also available in non-drip.	Very absorbent and needs protection from dirt. Not very resistant to wear and tear.
Same as matt emulsion but offers a faint sheen.	Quick to apply, dries quickly, and is more hard-wearing than matt emulsion.	Less durable than oil-based counterparts and unlike matt emulsion –tends to show flaws.
Matt emulsion qualities with higher shine, for use on interior woodwork.	All the advantages of a water-based paint combined with the appearance and easy cleaning of a gloss finish.	Can only be used on interior surfaces. Not as long-lasting as an oil-based gloss.
For tinting water-based paints and glazes, and for stencilling.	Quick drying. Good colour range. Dries to a durable finish.	Even when a retarder is added, quick drying limits their use to smaller areas.
A tinted oil-based medium thinned with white spirit, it produces a slow-drying, durable top coat in decorative effects.	Exceptional covering power, which makes it relatively cheap. Dries slowly, giving time for it to be worked on. Provides a transparent coat.	Slow drying leaves it vulnerable for a long time. Tends to yellow when deprived of light (behind pictures and large pieces of furniture).
Tinted water-based medium that creates a quick-drying top coat in decorative paint effects.	Dries to a clear finish without yellowing.	Dries much more quickly than its oil-based counterpart.
Prepares raw wood for undercoat.	Contains more oil than undercoats and seals the wood, which is porous.	Liable to take a long time to dry.
Well known for car repairs and suitable for a wide variety of applications, principally on small items.	Very quick drying due to high solvent content. Works with a thin coat. Good for stencils and for providing a smoky effect.	Very expensive and cannot be applied over oil-based mediums. Highly inflammable and can be difficult to apply evenly.
Protects most surfaces, including wall, floors, woodwork and smaller items.	Versatile and hard-wearing. Widely available and offered in matt, satin and gloss.	Tends to have a yellow tint. Hard when dry, and therefore difficult to rub down.
A quick-drying size used in gilding to stick the metal leaf to the ground.	Dries very quickly, lessening the risk of debris contaminating the surface.	Because it dries so quickly it tends to be brittle and give the leaf less glow than slower sizes.
Primarily for French polishing. The shellac known as knotting makes a useful barrier coat to prevent bleeding of colours and seals knots in new wood.	Dries very quickly and has a solvent base that makes it a successful isolating layer between coats.	Has a relatively short storage time and is not resistant to water or alcohol.

Glazes

A wash is merely powder colour suspended in a solution of water. Prior to its application the surface must be rubbed with chalk dust or whiting to remove any oil or grease. When dry, washes remain vulnerable and should be protected by a varnish as soon as possible. Thinned-down emulsion can make a good colour wash. The problem that often arises with an emulsion wash, however, is that the edge dries too quickly and spoils the effect. This can be solved by adding a spoonful of glycerine to each half-litre of emulsion wash, which will prolong the drying time.

A water-based glaze or PVA (polyvinyl acetate) medium is a polymer emulsion that may be diluted with water. When allowed to dry, it forms a clear transparent film which is extremely resistant to yellowing. These glazes must be tinted with a good quality water-soluble pigment. Emulsion glaze can be mixed with a coloured emulsion or latex paint to match a scheme or design, but the opaque mix will flatten the effect.

Emulsion glazes are extremely useful, retaining the benefits of transparency without the difficulties of yellowing. When dry they are water-resistant, and they are available in matt, satin and gloss finishes. The fact that they are water-based eases the problem of cleaning brushes and equipment, but means that drying times are not long enough for some finishes to be achieved with them. This book shows the best and easiest way of doing each technique.

Oil-based glazes
A glaze is a transparent layer of paint tinted with an artists' oil or stainer, and applied over another glaze or ground of a different colour to modify it. Glazes have been used in oil painting for centuries to give depth and a wonderful translucent glow. The glazes that are manufactured today have changed little over the years and contain a high proportion of linseed oil. Oil glazes can provide the most wonderful finishes, but they do have one potentially major drawback – the linseed oil gives them a propensity to yellow.

In the early 1980s the resurgence of paint effects inspired artisans to embrace a wide range of decorative effects without fully understanding their qualities. As a result, powder blue glazes became green in a matter of weeks, and walls yellowed badly, especially when the finish was deprived of light, behind furniture or pictures, for example.

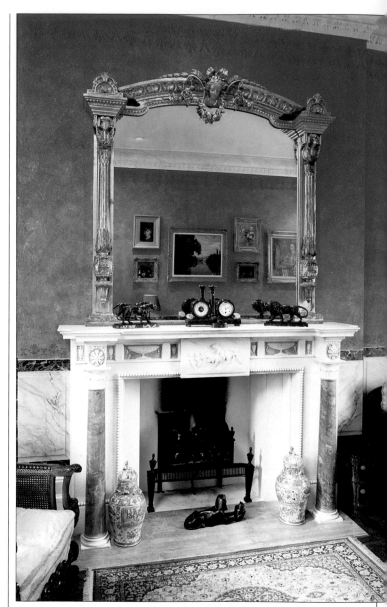

PETER FARLOW
▲ The rich glowing tones of this sumptuous room could only be achieved by using a glaze. The walls have been scumbled (a loose form of colour wash) in a magnificent red. Stencilled patterns, the bottom line cleverly echoing the top, add elegance and prevent the red from becoming overwhelming. A dado rail in dark marble enhances the majesty of the red and links it with the beautifully marbled panels designed to reflect the marble columns of the fire surround.

▶ An oil based glaze (right) has turned yellow (left). All oil-based glazes, particularly pale colours, have a propensity to yellow. However, you can prevent or delay yellowing by taking certain precautions.

Today, decorators are aware of the problem and, although a certain degree of yellowing will eventually occur, it can be reduced and delayed for a considerable time. This is especially important where pastel colours are applied on large areas, such as walls. First, be sure to use a good quality artists' oil or universal stainer. Cheap colours may initially look the same as their expensive counterparts, but their light-fastness – that is, their permanence – and their strength of purity are bound to be less acceptable. When mixing colour and glaze, make sure you concoct a strong mix. This is not as obvious as it sounds. The glaze is transparent, and so is the colour you are adding to it. Only by painting a patch will you be able to tell its strength.

Some people feel that a true glaze should be thinned to the right consistency and then applied to create the finish. Any yellowing that occurs should be accepted as a price worth paying for the effect achieved. Others prefer a finish that is not only decorative, but serviceable with a reasonably long life. As a result, they add white oil-based paint or undercoat to

Mixing colours

the glaze. This reduces its transparency and slightly flattens the finish, but it also retards any yellowing.

Adopting this route, allows you to to take a short-cut. Instead of tinting your glaze with colour and then adding white paint, you can add a pre-tinted undercoat or eggshell to the glaze. This reduces mixing time and offers you the extra ability to colour-match or tone with a range of pre-mixed colours. If undercoat is used, the ratio should be approximately 20 per cent paint to 80 per cent glaze. For eggshell oil-based paint, use 30 per cent paint to 70 per cent glaze, because eggshell is more transparent than undercoat. The mix should now be thinned by approximately 20 per cent spirit to 80 per cent. This should result in a coloured glaze with the consistency of single cream, which is ready to be applied.

SAFETY WITH GLAZES

Care is essential when using oil-based glazes. The thinned mix will have a very much higher spirit content than paint and will therefore give off more fumes. Make sure your working area is well-ventilated and prohibit smoking. Spread out rags which you have used for cleaning brushes or to achieve a finish and which have become saturated with glaze and leave them out to dry. They must not be disposed of while still wet, as due to their low flash point, there is a danger of spontaneous combustion. Finally, although the oil content will prolong drying time, you should optimize conditions by keeping the temperature and humidity as constant as possible throughout.

Although a paint stockist can mix most of the colours you are likely to need, mixing your own colours is very satisfying and means that you can achieve the exact shade you have in mind. Also, many artists' paints are mixtures of colours, and will therefore have lost much of their clarity. By mixing pure pigments – in powder, tube or tin form – with oil- or water-based paints or glazes you will be better able to achieve the right degree of transparency.

Blues
Ultramarine is nearest to the primary blue of the colour circle. It is a pure colour with a high tinting strength. To retain its clarity when mixing, combine it with viridian for a blue-green, or alizarin red for the purest of violets. Prussian blue is an ultra-powerful tint. Even a tiny trace will turn yellows and browns into bright green. It goes muddy with reds, however, except cadmium red with which it makes a rich deep black. Cobalt blue is midway between a transparent and an opaque colour, but is

easily swamped by other colours when mixed. Cerulean and blue-green oxide are both variations of cobalt.

Yellows

The most natural yellow pigments are the ochres obtained from clays, which have a naturally dulling effect. Synthetic versions of these (known as Mars colours) are slightly clearer and brighter, but are still classed as dulling colours. Cadmium yellow comes in countless tones, the deepest of which are the most opaque, but medium-tone cadmiums equal the primary yellow of the colour circle. Mixing with these destroys their clarity. Naples yellows have very strong covering power, so avoid these for glazing.

Reds

Like ochres, natural red pigments come from clays and their names and earth tones often reflect their origins. Cadmium reds, like the yellows, lose their brilliance when mixed. They are unsuitable for glazing, because the pigment remains in fine granules. Cadmium mixed with alizarin comes close to a primary red. Alizarin reds, like cadmiums, come in an endless variety of tones, from orange to violet. They make excellent glazes, especially over an opaque red or green, but if applied too thickly, alizarin loses its glow completely.

Greens

Viridian, which is very close to the spectrum colour, is cool and pure in tone. It is transparent and so brilliant that it retains this quality even when mixed with white. Chrome green is much more opaque and suitable as a ground colour.

The similarly coloured terre verte is appropriate for glazing, and is an ideal complement for red.

Browns

The umbers, raw and burnt, are the classic shadow colours. Burnt umber makes a good black when mixed with Prussian blue. It is heavy in tone and opaque – a good general darkener. Raw umber, having more water content, is more transparent. Raw sienna is transparent and makes a brilliant, light glaze. Burnt sienna is more opaque.

Points to consider

There are two stages in colour mixing: mixing the colour with the medium; and mixing one colour with another to achieve a match. The most important point to bear in mind when mixing any paint or glaze is that the two substances should be as near each other's viscosity as possible. If, for example, artists' oil colour were squeezed directly into a pot of transparent oil glaze and stirred, the colour would not all mix. A lump of pure colour would appear at the least expected moment and ruin the effect.

It is advisable to thin down all artists' colours before mixing. With oil colour, add a little white spirit or turpentine substitute and break the colour down into a thinner paste, using a brush or a palette knife. Add the spirit a little at a time, blending it thoroughly with each addition. Use the same technique for watercolour or acrylic colour, substituting

water for white spirit. Always use the artists' colours rather than the less expensive but lower quality students' ranges. Make sure that the colour has a reasonable permanence rating – no less than three stars. Good manufacturers issue catalogues that provide information on the performance of their colours and also indicate which are transparent and which are opaque.

The ideal colour-mix glaze will have the correct colour and depth, will be transparent, and will last the longest possible time without yellowing. However, it may not be possible to achieve all of these qualities simultaneously. For example, if the desired effect is only achievable with an oil-based glaze, and the chosen colour is a pale blue, you would either have to add white to reduce the yellowing qualities of the glaze, which would lessen its transparency, or the colour or finish would have to be changed. The only way around the pitfalls is careful planning.

If you don't feel ready for colour mixing, take a short-cut. Buy the appropriate colour of paint – either oil- or water-based – and add the relevant glaze in a ratio of approximately 25 per cent colour to 75 per cent glaze. In the case of oil, this mix should be thinned with white spirit by about 20 per cent. For emulsion glaze, the thinning will vary from finish to finish but approximately 10 per cent of water is normally added to the mix.

◄ **A selection of manufacturer's colour charts showing the huge range of colours, tints and shades available.**

Applied and subtractive finishes

Decorative finishes may involve adding paint or glaze to a surface, or removing it. An applied finish is added, usually to a dry surface. But when you apply a coat to a surface and then manipulate it in some way, you create a subtracted finish, because the paint or glaze is taken away in some areas to achieve the effect. The fundamental consideration when using a subtracted finish is drying time. The longer the paint stays wet, the longer it will be workable, but the longer it will be vulnerable too. A small surface, such as a box or picture frame, will take several hours to dry. In a larger area, such as a room, it is essential for the wet edge (see page 16) to advance across the surface without drying. It is therefore standard practice to split the operation into two parts. Complete alternate surfaces and carefully wipe each adjacent area clean of any overlap with a rag. Having allowed the first application to dry, you can work on the remaining walls without fear of accidental damage. To increase the speed of application, it is a good idea to enlist the help of another person, particularly while you are gaining experience.

An applied finish, such as sponging, or ragging on, is usually unaffected by drying time. In general, the quicker-drying water-based mediums are better for these. The great advantage to applied finishes is that there is no pressure – the process can be halted at any point and continued at a later date without undue risk to the finished effect. You can therefore attempt a large project without help.

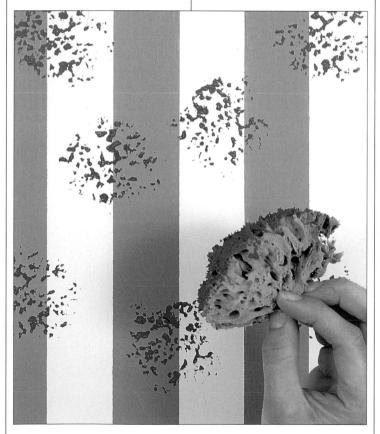

Applied finish – sponging on

Subtractive finish – rag rolling

Applying paints

The finish of your walls or woodwork will largely depend on how you apply the paint. Applying paint is not difficult, but if you keep the following advice in mind, the results will look more professional.

Types of paint
Undercoat is an oil-based paint which makes an excellent base for over-decorating techniques, as well as oil-based finishing coats. Matt emulsions have no sheen and are best suited to bumpy and old walls. Emulsions with a slight sheen are often called silk finish or semi-gloss. They do not absorb dirt so readily and are easier to sponge clean than matt emulsions, but they may reveal any flaws in the surface. Gloss paints are oil-based and usually applied to wood and metal.

Emulsion paint dries by evaporation of the water content, so keep the windows closed when applying it. Open the windows as soon as the work is completed. Most water-based paints can be given a further coat after approximately four hours,

depending on the temperature and humidity and the porosity of the surface.

Using a roller
When using a roller, ensure that it is evenly coated, then roll it in all directions, making your final strokes lighter in pressure to lessen the imprint of the roller pile. Use a 25 mm (1 in) brush for edges and intricate areas.

Using a brush
When using a brush for emulsion, apply the paint in all directions with long sweeping strokes to give a full level coat. Use a smaller brush of about 25 mm (1 in) to apply the paint behind pipes and other awkward areas. Begin at the top corner of a wall and work your way down in a patch width that you find comfortable. Do not stretch or reach while on a ladder – the time saved is not worth the danger.

When using a brush for gloss lay on generously over a small section and distribute evenly with cross-strokes. Finish by removing any excess paint and lay off with firm, even strokes.

Laying off
This term applies to the very last strokes of wet paint or varnish in any particular direction. Wipe your brush clean on the side of the tin or on the strike wire across the tin, then use long, even, extremely light strokes. If you are painting wood, the strokes should be in the direction of the grain. The aim of laying off is to eliminate any brush marks or at least to reduce them.

PAINTING ORDER

The usual order when painting a room is ceiling, walls, woodwork. When painting ceilings or walls, begin with an edge and work in sections, trying not to overlap. Painting should always be done methodically, but quickly, keeping the wet edge moving, so that one section does not dry before the edges are blended with the next section.

Painting order is particularly important when it comes to windows and doors. The diagrams show the correct sequence.

Door and frame

Casement window   **Sash window**

Preparation

Surfaces

Surfaces

◆

Sanding

New bare plaster

Ensure that new plaster is absolutely dry before applying paint to it. Water trapped in the plaster weakens the adhesion of the paint and may cause blistering. Some plasters have an alkaline nature, and when the plaster dries, white fluffy alkaline crystals may be deposited on the surface. These should be removed with a dry brush before painting. It is important to dry-brush the plaster anyway before painting to remove any surface dirt.

Fill any cracks or holes with a plaster-based or cellulose-based filler, dampening the area slightly first with a little water. For the best results, overfill the hole or crack so that it is proud of the surface and overlaps the surrounding area. When it is thoroughly dry, level out the filler using a medium- and then fine-grade sandpaper and block. The sanding block is the best means of achieving an even surface. Always begin with a medium to coarse grade of sandpaper to remove most of the filler, and progress to a finer paper. Never use a paper coarser than the previous one. Only use sandpaper when cutting back filler, not on raw plaster walls: however fine the paper, it will make scratches. Remove nibs (rough flecks) and plaster splashes with a scraper, holding it flat against the surface and sliding it gently to avoid digging into the plaster.

Preparation should be compatible with the finished effect: oil-based for an oil-based finish and water-based for a water-based effect. For a finish using a water-based glaze or a wash, prepare the plaster with a coat of emulsion or latex, thinned half and half with water. This thin coat seals the surface and creates a film which is absorbed by the plaster. Many modern paints tend to lie on top of the plaster rather than penetrating it. The sealer coat bridges the gap between plaster and paint, ensuring better adhesion throughout.

When the sealer coat is dry, any flaws in the surface will become apparent, and further filling will be necessary. This is best done with a fine-surface vinyl-based filler. Use very fine glasspaper to avoid breaking the paint surface, together with a sanding block for a true finish. Before recoating the wall with a full-strength emulsion or latex, quickly touch in the filled areas with the full-strength paint. This will save a complete coat to conceal them later on.

Old plaster

If you have stripped off wallpaper, it is important to remove any trace of paste or size remaining on the surface, because these can cause the newly applied paint to flake. Wash the wall with warm water and sugar soap. Be sure to rinse off all the soap before leaving to dry, when a light sanding with a fine glasspaper will ensure your surface is clean. Fill the holes and cracks in

**Sanding block
with glasspaper**

17

the same way as for new plaster.

Now you need to assess the quality of the surface and make a choice. On a poor surface, it is often more economical to line the walls with heavy-duty lining paper (600 grade) than to spend hours laboriously filling and sanding. If you decide against paper, continue following the procedure for new plaster.

Lining paper should be butt-jointed, and not overlapped, to avoid a seam. The porous paper will act in a similar way to the raw plaster, so even if the end effect is to be oil-based, the paper should be sealed with a thinned emulsion or PVA solution. The paper will soak this up and appear rather furry. When dry, it should be lightly sanded with a fine-grained glasspaper in readiness for the next coat. This will be water- or oil-based, depending on the base to be used for your final effect.

Painted plaster
The preparation in this instance is simply to ensure that the surface is clean, and that the paint to be applied will have some form of "key" to adhere to. Wash the area from top to bottom with a mild soap solution, taking care to rinse it clean. Treat any mould with a commercial fungicide. Key the surface by sanding with a medium-grade sandpaper or medium- to coarse-grade wet-and-dry paper, in conjunction with your sanding block.

As usual, the final effect will dictate which type of paint you now apply. If you plan to use oil glazes, apply two or three coats of an oil-based undercoat in the appropriate colour, followed by a coat of oil-based eggshell. If the final effect is to be achieved with a water-based paint or glaze, apply unthinned emulsion directly onto the wall.

It is a temptation to apply paint too thickly in an effort to finish this boring part of the exercise. But it is far better to paint thinly, so that drying is quicker, and there is less time to wait between coats. In some cases the pigments used in paints are unstable and "bleed" through – red being the commonest offender. One or two coats of aluminium primer will act as a barrier and solve this problem.

Preparation over wallpaper
You might consider painting over wallpaper for one of two reasons. Firstly,

Sanding block with wet-and-dry paper

Scraper

because you wish to retain the paper's texture, or secondly, you fear that the plaster behind the paper is in such bad repair that most of it would be removed with the paper. Check that the paper is well stuck, with no peeling edges. Pull off any loose pieces, and fill all gaps and joints with a vinyl-based filler.

Don't be tempted to size old wallpaper, as any water-based solution will cause it to swell and create wrinkles and blisters. Apply an oil-based primer or thin undercoat and allow to dry.

Paint often causes colour to bleed from wallpaper. This can be prevented by applying an aluminium primer or thin coat of knotting, diluted with methylated spirit to seal the colour in. Continue with the application of the base coats as before.

Concrete floors
To prepare a concrete floor for finishing, first clean with a mild detergent and rinse. When dry, surface-fill with a fine-grade filler. Smooth the dried filler with a scraper, and apply a couple of coats of linoleum paint to the floor, lightly sanding between coats.

Pottery and earthenware
Any pottery or earthenware which has not been glazed is extremely porous, and requires sealing. Two coats of PVA are therefore needed before you apply the ground or base coat.

Glass
This must be clean and free from any grease. To make sure of this, wash the glass in warm soapy water and rinse it thoroughly. Form a key by using wet-and-dry paper, together with a little water. The water acts as a lubricant and keeps the grit of the paper from getting clogged. Apply two or three coats of oil-based undercoat, followed by the appropriately coloured eggshell. Emulsion (latex) or water-based paints and glazes are not recommended for use on glass and ceramics. Being less durable, they are prone to chip and lose their grip on the surface.

Wire brushes

Metal surfaces

Old objects are often affected by rust. Never try to paint over even the smallest sign of rust, as this will merely recur and spoil the finish. Every trace of rust must be removed. For small areas use steel wool. For a large area you will need a wire cup brush or scouring wheel attached to an electric drill. There are many ways to deal with rust, and the refinishing products sold for cars can be a great help. If the piece is damaged, you could mend holes with a fibreglass repair kit after all the rust has been removed.

Non-ferrous metals, such as aluminium or copper, should be washed with white spirit before priming.

New tin pieces should be washed in a half-and-half mixture of white vinegar and water to remove the greasy protective coating. Once the object has been cleaned, you can prime it with its appropriate primer. When this is dry, apply two coats of undercoat followed by two coats of eggshell. Emulsion, water-based paints and glazes are not recommended on this surface.

Raw wood

Raw wood must first be cleaned of grease and dust. Wipe it down with a mild detergent solution. Take care not to drench the wood, as this could lead to warping. Leave overnight to dry. The grain will rise due to the dampening and must now be sanded. Choose your grit carefully. If the wood is rough, a coarse paper is required. If the piece has been made by a cabinet maker, considerably finer paper will be needed. On flat areas use a sanding block, and remember to sand in the direction of the grain. Start at one side of the area and use long strokes of firm, balanced pressure. Overlap the sanding strips so that you do not miss anything. Use your sense of touch, and as you finish each area, wipe clean with a tack rag.

Treat all raw wood as if it still contained running sap. Any knot or crack that may bleed sap must be sealed with wood knotting. This consists of shellac (a resin) in a methylated spirit base, and dries very quickly indeed. Because of this it is prone to crack, and therefore requires two or three coats over and just beyond the knot or crack. Any holes that need filling should be treated in the same way to prevent the stopper drying out too quickly and becoming weak.

Next, apply a good-quality universal primer, making sure that the paint floods into any fault and seals the wood completely. Take extra care over the end grain, which will be more porous than the other areas. Once this coat is dry, you can stop and fill.

Once the filler has dried, sand it flush with the surface. Clean the work again with a tack rag before applying the undercoat.

Undercoat is normally put on with a brush. However, on especially large areas, it can be helpful to use a roller. Do not choose a foam roller for this – or for any oil-based paint – as it may be adversely affected by the white spirit in the paint. The aim when applying any base paint is to achieve a dense, even finish with the least amount of imperfections. As with emulsion or latex, oil-based paints should be applied so as to limit the size of the wet edge (see page 16). On vertical surfaces it helps to lay off (see page 16) or lightly brush the paint in an upward direction.

Once the undercoat is dry, lightly wipe the area with a fine-grade abrasive paper to remove any dust particles which have adhered to the paint and to create a key for the next coat. A second undercoat is normally necessary, followed by two coats of eggshell of your chosen colour. After each coat dries, whisk over the surface quickly with a fine abrasive paper to remove any particles and to key in the next coat.

Previously treated surfaces

As with any refinishing work, the previous treatment must be assessed. Firstly, is the existing finish in good condition? And secondly, is it compatible with the intended effect? If the answers to these two questions are both positive, then all that is required is to clean and key the surface before going on with the base coats.

Wax is not compatible with paint, so if your surface has been polished with wax, this needs to be removed. For waxed timber, use methylated spirit and a medium (00) wire wool. Remember to work with the grain of the wood and, when most of the wax has been removed, go over the surface again using a cloth in place of the wool. If you are dealing with a highly polished surface, use a finer wire wool – 000 or even 0000. Oiled wood should be treated in a similar way to waxed timber. Replace the methylated spirit with mineral or white spirit and use a 00 wire wool. If the surface has been varnished or shellacked and is in good condition, all you need to do is clean and key it in before applying the base coat.

If the surface is chipped or flaking it should be removed. This can be done with abrasives such as sandpaper, or with a commercial stripper. Use abrasives if at all possible, because most strippers will remove oil from the wood, causing it to dry and weaken. A blow lamp with a paint stripper head can be effective. Be careful to play the flame from side to side to avoid charring the wood.

A French-polished surface should be treated in a similar way to waxed timber, with methylated spirit and medium (00) and fine (0000) wire wool. Swab the surface with the methylated spirit first, then

▼ **Wire wool is available in fine and coarse grades.**

rub it with medium-grade wire wool. The polish will soften quite quickly, and you will be able to wipe it off the surface. Once you have roughly cleaned the object in this way, go over it again with the fine wire wool and spirit, remembering to work with the grain.

Gesso

Gesso is a mixture of whiting, or powdered chalk, and glue (see recipe right). It is used to fill the grain of wood and to provide a smooth hard ground for gold leaf, marbling or japan work (a lacquer or varnish finish). A surface prepared with gesso will be smooth and cool to the touch like marble. Begin by giving the surface a coat of glue size or PVA to prevent the glue in the gesso being absorbed by the timber. Secondly, punch and fill any pins or nails which may interfere with the adhesion of the gesso. Strengthen any joints by smoothing thin pieces of linen or silk soaked in gesso over them. These cloth reinforcements, which are called *intelaggio*, reduce the tendency of the gesso to crack, and should be left for at least two days to dry.

Brush the gesso on smoothly and evenly to avoid bubbles. Most pieces will need six or seven coats. The first few coats will be relatively slow in drying, as the coats build up they will dry faster. The correct time to apply the next coat of gesso is when its predecessor has become dull and is firm enough to be brushed without being disturbed. If a coat is

allowed to dry completely, the fusion between it and the next coat will be weakened and prone to chip. Once you start gessoing, you should continue until the piece is completed. Never increase the temperature of a room to reduce drying time, as this will make the gesso brittle. Remember when mixing your gesso always to overestimate quantities. It is far better to throw some away than to have to stop in the middle of application to make more. In fact, if the ratio of glue size to whiting varies much, adhesion may suffer. When the gesso has dried thoroughly, which normally takes two or three days, the surface will be ready for recutting and repolishing.

Recutting, which further smoothes and prepares the surface, is generally done with a cabinet scraper. This is a stiff, square-edged piece of steel, which has a slight burr on the edge. The scraper is held so that it leans slightly in the direction to which it is pushed or pulled. Work the area in a lattice pattern so that lines are not missed.

Water polishing makes the top surface of the gesso into a thin paste, which fills any superficial flaws. Dampen a clean cotton cloth and wring it out. Stretch the cloth over your fingers or over a sanding block and rub the surface. The porous gesso will soak up the water readily, and the cloth will require redampening frequently. Do not allow the surface to become too wet, or the crispness achieved by

MIXING YOUR OWN GESSO

- 45 gm (1½ oz) rabbit-skin glue (granules or powder)
- Whiting (powdered chalk)
- Sieve
- Wooden spoon
- Saucepan
- Jar or other container

Soak the glue overnight in 750 ml (1¼ pt) of water. Warm the resulting gel in a jar or bain marie until it liquefies. Do not allow it to boil. Skim off any scum that forms on the surface or it will make lumps. Add enough whiting through a sieve to achieve a consistency similar to that of single cream. Stir the liquid with a wooden spatula or spoon so that all lumps are smoothed away. The gesso is now ready to be applied. On average, 280 ml (10 fl oz) of size will require approximately 620 ml (22 fl oz) of whiting. Depending on the thickness of application 240 ml (8 fl oz) will cover a 1.2 m- (4 ft-) square panel.

recutting will be blurred. When the surface is smooth, leave the piece to dry for at least 24 hours.

A coat of shellac is normally sufficient to seal the gesso prior to applying the ground coat.

Sanding

This is an essential task which is often overlooked. Many wonderful finishes are marred by lack of attention to touch. After all, a beautiful marble cries out to be touched, and if time and effort have been expended to achieve such an effect, it seems odd not to add the little extra effort that can turn a mediocre finish into a joy to view *and* touch. Sanding is probably the most important operation in preparation. It must be done to remove tool marks, and to smooth the surface and round the edges in readiness for paint. By using the correct procedures and selected grades of abrasive paper, you can achieve an extremely high standard of finish. Sanding can be divided into three stages: using a coarse grade to create a new surface or shape; followed by a medium paper to smooth down the new surface; and using the finest grades to ready the surface for polish. In preparing wood, be careful to sand with the grain.

Wet-and-dry paper is dark grey and, as the name implies, can be used wet or dry. The advantage of this is that a lubricant can be used to keep the paper sharp. With glasspaper the surface grit often becomes clogged and you have to change to a fresh piece. A lubricant (normally water) prevents clogging and therefore extends the life of the paper. When using wet-and-dry paper with a lubricant, rinse the surface regularly and make sure that all the sludge is removed. Only use wet-and-dry paper with a lubricant on a painted surface or metal – never on raw unsealed wood.

Silicon carbide paper is a crystalline abrasive that is very hard and sharp. It may be used on lacquers, plastics, wood, composition materials (for example, medium density fibreboard), plaster and metal.

1 **Silicon carbide**
2 **Glasspaper**
3 **Garnetpaper**

ABRASIVE PAPERS FOR SANDING

GLASSPAPER	GARNET-PAPER	SILICON CARBIDE
–	–	12/0–600
–	–	11/0–500
–	10/0–400	10/0–400
–	9/0–320	9/0–320
–	8/0–280	8/0–280
–	7/0–240	7/0–240
00	6/0–220	6/0–220
0	4/0–150	4/0–150
1	3/0–120	3/0–120
1½	2/0–100	2/0–100
F2	1/0–80	1/0–80
M2	½–60	½–60
S2	1	1
2½	1½	1½
3	2	2
–	2½	2½
–	3	3
–	3½	3½

More important than the type of abrasive paper is the size of grit. This is graded by numbers which rise as the grit becomes finer. The paper most commonly found in DIY stores will be labelled coarse, medium and fine. This is a good base from which to start. However, as you progress with your project, you will discover the need for a finer and maybe harder paper. By using the appropriate grit grade, you can obtain far more rewarding effects. The golden rule when sanding, however, is always to make a gradual transition from coarse to fine. Work with the same or a finer paper but never a coarser one, because this will cause scratches. The table (left) will help you choose the most suitable paper and grade.

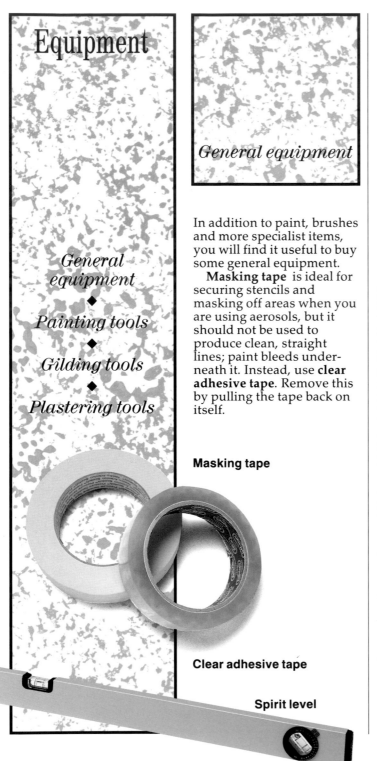

Equipment

General equipment

- General equipment
  ◆
- Painting tools
  ◆
- Gilding tools
  ◆
- Plastering tools

In addition to paint, brushes and more specialist items, you will find it useful to buy some general equipment.

Masking tape is ideal for securing stencils and masking off areas when you are using aerosols, but it should not be used to produce clean, straight lines; paint bleeds underneath it. Instead, use **clear adhesive tape**. Remove this by pulling the tape back on itself.

Masking tape

Clear adhesive tape

Spirit level

Palette knives

Scalpel

Steel tape measure

Tack rag

A **spirit level** and a **plumb-line** are two of the most essential decorating tools, with uses ranging from checking that new plaster is level to ensuring shelves are up straight. A steel **tapemeasure** is used for a variety of purposes from measuring to providing a cutting edge.

Cutting mats, tracing paper and **scalpels** are primarily useful for stencils or découpage.

Goggles and **dust masks** are both important safety items. Wear goggles whenever there is a danger of splashing paint, medium or varnish into your eyes. Wear a dust mask when sanding, or using powders.

Dust sheets are essential whenever you need to protect the floor or any other item. **Cotton rags** are useful for lifting off glazes, creating effects and cleaning brushes, etc. **Mutton cloth** is a variable-weave cloth used for cleaning up and creating various paint effects. **Tack rags** are tacky open-weave rags, ideal for cleaning surfaces prior to painting or varnishing.

Many people paint out of the tin, but a **paint kettle** allows you to use a small amount of paint at one time, keeping the remainder clean and protected from air (which causes a skin to form). **Palette knives** are good for breaking up artists' oil colour when mixing a glaze. A **painter's mate** is extremely useful for painting corners or other adjacent surfaces.

Goggles

Cutting mat and tracing paper

Dust mask

Plumb-line

Cotton rags

Dust sheet

Mutton cloth

Paint kettle

Painting tools

There is a vast range of brushes available. The brushes listed here will cover most of your decorating needs.

Standard decorators' brushes are part of any painter's kit. Sizes will vary depending on whether you are applying gloss or emulsion. **Radiator brushes** will make painting radiators a great deal easier.

Artist's brushes come in different shapes and are composed of different hair, ranging from the best and most expensive sable through squirrel and ring cat to more affordable hog hair. **Round** brushes have a fine point and should always be reshaped after cleaning. **Flats**, which have a square end, produce wide, thin imprints. **Filberts** are also flat but gently taper to a conical shape. **Fans** are just as they sound – splayed out like an open fan.

Badger-hair softeners are probably the most important members of a specialist collection. Badger-hair brushes are very expensive indeed, but once you have experienced using one for marbling or graining, you will find the

23

effect hard to equal. Nevertheless, it would be wise to learn how to soften using a **hog-hair softener** or dusting brush before trying a badger. This is because it is easy to produce an acceptable effect with a badger brush, and you will therefore have less incentive to improve your technique.

Dusting brushes are also known as jam dusters or, when a pale bristle is used, lily-bristle dusters. These brushes were originally designed to remove dust from an area prior to coating. They have been largely replaced for this purpose by the tack rag, except for removing deposits from mouldings and intricate areas. More often they serve as softeners or for stippling in small- to medium-sized areas.

Fitches are the decorator's closest equivalent to an artist's brush, and are used for small-scale work, such as cutting in the glazing bars of a window. They are available in hog hair or lily bristle, and in fan, oval, flat or angled shapes. The angled fitch is often used for spattering because of its shape and its stiff bristles.

Floggers and **draggers** are used for graining. They come in various sizes. Draggers are primarily used for dragging and floggers for flicking against wet glaze.

Mops are soft brushes of squirrel or camel hair used when gilding, primarily to remove surplus gold or metal leaf, and to apply gold powder.

Mottlers or spalters are available in squirrel, hog hair, and even sable. These are graining brushes, used for figuring or drawing the grain, normally after the undergraining is complete.

Stencil brushes are designed to achieve a fine effect when stippling over a stencil. They are made from hard-wearing bristle which has some spring, and are available in different sizes.

Sword brushes or sword liners were originally used just for lining. It has long soft hair and an angled face which enable it to travel long distances without having to be replenished. Now it is more often used for veining in marbling. Care must be taken to reshape it after washing.

Stippling brushes come in a variety of sizes. They are comparatively expensive and should be cleaned and stored carefully.

Lily-bristle dusting brush

Hog-hair softener

Dragger

Flogger

Stippling brush

Stencil brushes

Mop

Sword liner

Emulsion brush

Standard decorators' brushes

Badger-hair softener

Radiator brush

Standard paint brush

Mottler

1. Nylon flat
2. Nylon round
3. Nylon rigger
4. 5. 6. Nylon liners

Selection of round and flat fitches

Selection of sable, hog-hair and nylon brushes

BRUSH CARE

New brushes should be washed in warm water to remove loose bristles, and allowed to dry. This process should be repeated once or twice, or until no further bristles are lost. This is particularly important for varnish brushes. Remember that paint glaze or varnish dries on rollers and brushes just as easily as on walls. If you have to stop midway through it is important not to let the equipment dry out. If you are using oil-based glazes and paints, stand the brushes and rollers in enough water to cover them, thereby preventing the air from reaching them. Shake the brushes and rollers clear of water before restarting work. When using emulsion glaze or paint, never soak the equipment in water, because this will thin the paint or glaze that they contain. Depending on the length of your break, either wash the equipment and leave it to dry, or wrap the brushes and rollers in plastic film.

CLEANING BRUSHES – OIL

First, remove the majority of paint or glaze from the brush with a rag or paper towel. When using brush cleaner or white spirit, rinse the brush, using an old steel comb or wire brush to loosen stubborn colour. Always smooth or squeeze the bristles in a downward direction away from the stock. Once the brush appears to be clean of colour, it should be cleaned of solvent, but be sure that no paint remains on the brush before you do this. If you have used brush cleaner, rinse the brush clean in tepid water. White spirit can be removed with normal soap and lukewarm water. Do not use detergents as these tend to deprive the bristles of their natural oils. Shake the brush in order to remove as much water as possible, and either lay it on its side or place it, bristles upward, in a jar to dry. If you find that the bristles are starting to splay out, wrap them, when damp, in a collar of card secured with rubber band or sticky tape.

CLEANING BRUSHES – WATER

An emulsion glaze or latex paint is far more difficult to remove when dry than its oil-based counterparts. For this reason, try to wash the brushes and rollers used with this medium as soon as possible. A comb and a wire brush are useful tools when loosening thick, heavily-clogged bristles, but these should be wielded with care, and plenty of water should be used to flush the paint or glaze away. Dry and store the brushes in the same way as those used with oil-based paints and glazes.

Other painting equipment
Paint trays and **rollers** are part of every painter's kit. Do not use a foam roller for oil-based paint as it may be adversely affected by the white spirit in the paint.

Feathers can be used in marbling, as an alternative to fine artist's brushes or sword liners. Any clean and reasonably sturdy feather will do.

Graining rollers or rocker combs are available in different widths and grades. They are normally made of rubber and pulled across the wet glaze with a gentle rocking motion to produce a heart grain wood effect.

Combs come in rubber, leather and steel. A triangular rubber comb with differently graded teeth is a useful first choice.

It is important to choose the right **sponge** for your effect. Natural sponges are expensive, but will swell when immersed in water. Synthetic sponges have a regular shape but can be torn into more ragged and manageable pieces.

Swan and goose feathers

Rubber comb

Steel combs

Graining rollers

Marine and synthetic sponges

Check roller

Paint tray and roller in sleeve

MAKING A COMB

Manufactured combs are usually made of rubber, leather or steel, but you can make your own from virtually any strong material. Solid card is the easiest, but thick plastics – although harder to cut – will last longer. The squeegee used for cleaning windows can be adapted by cutting teeth into the rubber blade. The size of the comb will depend on the area to be finished – for a floor this might be up to 30 cm (12 in). The teeth need to be strong and flat to collect the glaze. Cut them with a craft knife or scissors, depending on the material.

Gilding tools

Gilder's cushion, knife and tip

Tools for plastering

Gold leaf is available from specialist suppliers and, like solid gold, its purity is measured in carat. The leaf most often used by professional gilders is 22 carat. This is available in different weights and thicknesses, referred to as standard or single, double and triple gold.

Silver leaf is sold in slightly larger leaves than gold. It is heavier and less expensive but, unlike gold, it tarnishes, and must be varnished. The leaf needs to be kept tightly wrapped to protect it from the air, and it should be trimmed before application to prevent the joints from showing up as darker strips.

Aluminium leaf is cheap and is supplied in large leaves, which makes application much quicker. Although greyer than silver, it can be used to great effect.

Schlag, or **Dutch, leaf** is an alloy of copper and zinc, and is available in shades of gold. It is far cheaper than gold, but needs varnishing to prevent it from tarnishing and, like silver leaf, should be kept wrapped.

Bronze powders, which range from pale gold to dark, or penny, bronze, can be used in their powdered form. Alternatively, you can mix them with a medium, such as gold size, to produce an effective paint.

Gold and other metal leaf is supplied in transfer or loose-leaf form. Transfer leaf is attached to thin tissue paper, so you can convey it to the surface easily without special tools.

Loose leaf is sold in books, as is transfer leaf, but because they are loose, you must take care to avoid the leaves falling out. As there is no backing to help you manipulate the leaf, you will need a **gilder's cushion**, a **knife** and a **tip** to convey it to the surface.

MAKING A POUNCE BAG

A pounce bag is a small cotton bag filled with whiting. It is used to dust the whiting over a surface in effects such as gilding, where it prevents unwanted adhesion of goldleaf, or graining, where it prepares an oil ground to receive a wash. To make the bag, take an old piece of fine cotton measuring about 20 cm (8 in) square and spread it out flat. Carefully put a tablespoonful of whiting into the middle of the square, and gather up the four corners. Secure the ends with string as low down as possible so as to make a neat tight bag.

A **spot board** is merely a strong clean board which is used to hold the mixed plaster. It should be placed so that it overhangs a bench or stool enough for you to hold the hawk under the edge of it when collecting plaster for use. The **hawk** is a small board, about 30 cm (12 in) square, with a short stick handle fixed to the underside. It is used to carry the plaster from the spot board to the surface, and to hold the plaster as you work. Use the **laying-on trowel** to apply the plaster and to spread it over the area.

Plastering bucket, hawk and trowel

Finishing

Varnishing

♦

Wax finishing

Varnishing

There are three main reasons for contemplating varnishing: to protect a completed effect; to provide a barrier; and to add depth and tactility to a finish. There are situations, therefore, that do not require varnish. But when varnish is needed, it is important to select the right one. There are probably as many types of varnish as there are paint, and each is tailored to suit a particular application.

Oil varnish
It would be impossible to list all the available varnishes, as new products are constantly being made, but these will usually be improved versions of

◀ **Specialist varnish brushes hold more liquid and are therefore recommended for large surfaces. A good-quality new paintbrush can be used for small surfaces.**

existing types. Probably the most robust – apart from industrial two-pack or acid catalyst lacquers – oil varnish is a higher build varnish than its water-based counterparts, but it does have a tendency to yellow. This needs to be taken into consideration, when the effect to be covered is fairly pale.

The easiest oil varnish to use is polyurethane. It gives a slightly hard and clinical finish compared with more traditional varnishes, but this can be modified by polishing, and is a small price to pay for its durability.

Oil varnishes can normally be purchased in three finishes: matt, which has almost no shine; satin, also called semi-gloss, which has a sheen; and gloss, which has a high sheen. Durability goes hand in hand with the finish: the higher the shine, the more protection offered.

If you want the protection but not the shine of a gloss finish, apply further coats of satin or matt varnish over the gloss. Be sure to key in by sanding before coating to ensure good adhesion. Several thin coats of varnish achieve a more even surface than one or two thick ones. Thinning the varnish with white spirit or turpentine substitute will aid application of the first two coats.

Water-based varnishes and sealers
Acrylic and vinyl-based resins suspended in water do not yellow, and offer some protection to the

Matt finish

Satin finish

Gloss finish

effect. PVA is probably best known as a glue, but also serves as a paint medium or size, and makes a useful sealer and varnish. The varnish can be thinned with water and, although it is often opaque in liquid form, it will dry clear.

Sprays
Cellulose lacquer in aerosol form can work well on emulsion or water-based finishes. Beware, however, of using it with oil-based mediums and colours. The cellulose thinners which dilute the lacquer act like paint stripper on these. The finish must be entirely water-based – including the ground coat – to avoid damage. Be careful to read the advice given by the manufacturer and to follow all the necessary precautions. This type of lacquer is far more combustible than any other,

and therefore demands greater respect. It takes far less time to dry, than its counterparts and is much thinner. It offers only minimal protection, but will not yellow.

Varnish is sometimes found in aerosol form, but this is an expensive way of finishing a piece. The varnish will be much thinner than it would be out of a tin, which will reduce its build and its protective qualities. Again, the manufacturer's advice should be followed to the letter, and the varnishing area must be well ventilated. When using aerosols it is always best to tilt the surface upwards towards the spray so that you can keep the can vertical.

Preparation for varnishing
Varnish is highly vulnerable when wet. Not only will the

shine be marred by a hair or a piece of fluff, but the decorative effect which requires protection may be weakened by any foreign body which becomes stuck in the varnish. Cleanliness is the answer. Wear clothes that are free from wool or fluff, cover your hair, and prepare your working environment carefully by minimizing outside draughts and limiting movement in your chosen area. If the piece to be varnished is small, it is a good idea to shelter it underneath a cardboard box or similar screen. Remember to allow some air to enter the box or the varnish will remain wet longer.

The temperature and humidity of the room are also important. The varnish needs to be reasonably warm in order to flow correctly. In a humid atmosphere, there is a

danger of blooming. This can also happen to oil glaze and gives the surface a powdery look. It occurs as a result of already damp air entering into contact with the drying varnish or glaze, or when a drop in temperature causes condensation on the drying surface. The answer is to avoid humid conditions, and to maintain as constant a temperature as possible.

The surface to be varnished should be smooth and free of nibs. Remove all grease by wiping with a cloth and a little white spirit. Take the tack rag, straight from its sealed plastic bag and use it to clean the area meticulously, changing regularly to a clean fold.

Thoroughly mix the varnish with a clean stick or dowel – never shake it, as this will cause bubbles. Then decant the varnish into a pot with a "strike

Varnishing
1 Brush on the varnish, gently laying off so that the brush marks flow away.

2 After the varnish has dried for 24 hours, smooth down the surface with a block and fine-grade wet-and-dry paper, using water as a lubricant.

3 When the water becomes sludgy, wash the surface with clean water and a sponge.

wire" attached. In cold weather the varnish may require warming before decanting. Varnish is inflammable so never use a naked flame for this. Take off the lid, and place the tin in warm water for a few minutes. Remove the tin and stir the varnish with a clean stick. If it is still too thick, repeat the exercise using hot water.

Load the pre-washed brush with the decanted varnish and transfer this directly to a piece of brown paper without wiping the excess onto the strike wire. Work the brush over the paper, spreading the varnish. This expels air from the bristles and removes any last stray bristles. From now on the brush will remain wet.

When varnishing is complete, the brush must be stored in keeper varnish. Make this by mixing two-thirds of white spirit or turpentine substitute with one-third of varnish. Suspend the brush so that the solution covers the bristles completely, keeping them clean, supple and free of air. You can buy a pot which has clips to hold the brushes in position and which is also equipped with a dust cover. Alternatively, use an old clean varnish pot, drill a hole in the stock of the brush and pass a wire through it which will rest on the lip of the pot.

Varnishing technique
Because varnish is transparent, it is advisable to have a strong light source behind the piece so that you can constantly check the surface for the glint which tells you which areas have been coated and which missed. On a limited area, such as a small table-top, start at the centre of the panel and work outwards. When the surface is extensive enough to require re-loading of the brush, apply the varnish in strips, using the technique of moving the wet edge. Try not to overload the surface with varnish, which could result in runs or sags. These build up slowly and then appear as if by magic. Practice will help you discover just how much varnish to apply and how thinly you can brush it out without its breaking. Remember that you can thin the early coats a little to make application easier. Wipe the excess from the brush by means of the strike wire and not the edge of the tin. The wire forces the returning varnish to enter the container in a thin stream, helping to prevent bubbles. It also reduces the build-up of the tacky drips often found hanging like stalactites around the inside lip of varnish tins. In time, these break and fall into the varnish, rendering it unusable,

Stone effect finish
Oil varnish can be treated after application to impart a stone-like quality to the surface. Apply the varnish in the normal way, and while it is wet, scatter granulated sugar over the surface. This will sink into the varnish in varying degrees, and must be allowed to dry hard. After about 24 hours, wash the surface with warm soapy water. The sugar will dissolve, and the pock-marked texture will become apparent.

Wax finishing

Wax finishing can be achieved over varnish, shellac and lacquers. Prepare the surface by rubbing gently with 320 grit paper to remove nibs and flaws. Clean with a tack rag. Place a small amount of wax polish between several layers of cheesecloth, press it onto the surface and apply it in a circular motion. Leave to dry for 10 minutes. Then rub the dried wax hard with a clean soft cloth, first in a circular motion, and then along the grain. Leave for an hour and repeat the application.

Polishing with wax and wire wool
This is the commonest way of polishing marble effects, and a fine finish can only be achieved over at least two coats of varnish. The surface should be flattened off first, using fine wet-and-dry paper and a block with water as a lubricant. Using a 0000 wire wool and good-quality wax, rub the length of the surface in long straight strokes. Finally buff up the finish with a soft rag.

4 Clean with a tack rag to prepare the smoothed varnish for a further coat.

5 Apply the final coat of varnish using the same method as before.

Techniques

You need no prior knowledge of paint effects to achieve pleasing results. However, you will achieve more successful results if you have suitable equipment and, most important of all, if you have prepared your surface correctly and to a high standard. If you enjoy colour and the interactions of colours, all you need to know is that most paint effects rely on the play between foreground and background. If the contrast between the two is great, the resulting effect will be loud or bold. Soft, subtle effects are achieved by using similar colours with similar strengths for ground and top coats.

The finishes described here have been simplified as much as possible to reduce decorating costs and increase ease of application. As you become more experienced, you may want to move on to more difficult and complicated techniques. One of the exciting aspects of decorative paint effects is that there are always different ways of achieving effects and, no matter how long you've been graining or marbling, there will always be new tricks and shortcuts to learn.

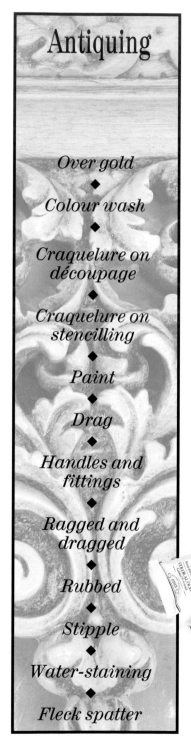

Antiquing

Over gold

◆

Colour wash

◆

*Craquelure on
découpage*

◆

*Craquelure on
stencilling*

◆

Paint

◆

Drag

◆

*Handles and
fittings*

◆

*Ragged and
dragged*

◆

Rubbed

◆

Stipple

◆

Water-staining

◆

Fleck spatter

Antiquing is a simulated ageing that can soothe a piece into its surroundings as well as creating an atmosphere of times gone by. The term applies to a myriad of techniques and effects, ranging from the pronounced distressing, or time-worn look, produced by a wire brush to the fine speckle of a spatter. Most effects achieved with a colour can also serve in antiquing. They cover applications as diverse as staining black-and-white prints with tea to ageing a new brass handle with boot polish.

The key to successful antiquing is subtlety. Where other effects ask to be noticed – even if elegance is their second name – antiquing needs the delicate tones and refined textures that will make a piece look as if it has been in situ for years. The colours normally used in antiquing are, therefore, rich, soft earth tones: raw umber, burnt umber, raw sienna, burnt sienna and ivory black.

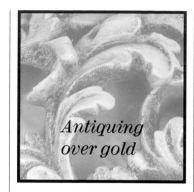

*Antiquing
over gold*

Gilding* is often antiqued, especially when applied to a classical design, where it may otherwise look too new and bright. First protect the gold with a thin tinted varnish* which will seal the piece and give some definition to carving. When the varnish is dry, use 000 or 0000 wire wool* to distress the piece. Concentrate on proud surfaces, edges and areas more prone to wear and tear. The gold will be removed in places, leaving the ground to show through. Once you have achieved a pleasing look choose a colour for the antiquing glaze.

Gilding is usually antiqued with burnt umber or burnt sienna, because they impart a rich glow which is bold enough to reduce the gold's power but retain a warmth which enhances the piece. Oil glaze is the preferable medium, as metal leaf can sometimes react with water to cause tarnishing.

Mix your chosen shade with the glaze to form a strong colour*. Apply the glaze liberally over the area and allow it a little time to adhere. Then stipple* or drag* the glaze with an open-weave cloth, such as mutton cloth*. This technique removes some of the glaze and ensures that all crevices and hollows have been thoroughly covered. Use a clean cotton rag, dampened with a little white spirit if necessary, to clean off the remaining glaze. Apply a varnish if you would like a sheen, but protection is not necessary, as natural wear and tear will merely add to the effect.

Equipment

*Pale oak varnish
Wire wool 000 or 0000
Oil glaze coloured with burnt
umber or burnt sienna
Varnish brush
Glaze brush
Mutton cloth
Cotton cloth
White spirit*

✱ Further information

Gilding *p.122*
Varnishing *p.29*
Equipment *p.22*
Colour mixing *p.13*
Stippling *p.104*
Dragging *p.54*

1 Having protected the gilded surface with a thin coat of pale oak varnish and allowed it to dry, rub over the surface with 000 or 0000 wire wool to give an impression of wear.

3 Using an open-weave cloth, such as mutton cloth, stipple and rub the glaze over the entire surface.

2 Mix the antiquing glaze – burnt sienna was the choice here – and apply it with a brush, taking care to penetrate all the details of the work.

4 Gently clean over the area with a clean soft cloth. In some instances it may be necessary to use a little white spirit to produce highlights.

5 The antiqued effect warms and softens the gilding; the finished object glows rather than standing out brashly.

6 When a heavier antique finish is needed, drag the glaze over the mouldings and carvings using mutton cloth and only the high points will appear as clean gold. The remainder will vary in tone according to its position.

Antiquing colour wash

Wood to be antiqued by the colour wash method* must be porous. If the piece has been colour washed and needs toning down, the technique can be continued without further ado. If the effect is to be applied to untreated wood, however, the surface must be cleaned with a mild detergent solution to remove any dirt or grease that may mar the finish. When choosing an antiquing colour, bear in mind the colour scheme of the surrounding area and the colour of the piece. The example here uses burnt umber. Although less hot than sienna used with the gold, this colour has the necessary warmth to counter the slight coldness of the green ground. The medium can be oil- or water-based. Oil gives more time for application and may, therefore, produce a less patchy effect.

Equipment
Oil- or water-based antiquing glaze with burnt umber
Brush
Rag

1 Apply the antiquing glaze to the unsealed wood. Brush the colour into the pores of the wood, flooding all the flaws and crevices.

2 Use an absorbent cloth to wipe the surface of any glaze not taken in by the wood. Rub quite hard, especially over proud areas, such as mouldings and edges.

3 The antiquing knocks back the strong green of the colour wash, giving an impression of age.

* Further information
Colour washing *p.47*

Antiquing découpage with craquelure

Découpage* often needs an effect which will consolidate and bind it. It can be antiqued in many ways but craquelure is one of the most effective. Craquelure is the French name for the network of fine cracks which often cover the surface of old oil paintings. The cracks are formed by the gradual and unequal shrinkage of neighbouring layers of paint under a varnish, and have become one of the tests of authenticity in an old painting.

The paint effect is achieved with two coats of varnish: a slow-drying oil-based coat and a quick-drying water-based one*. The oil-based varnish is applied first and when it has formed a skin the quick-drying water-based varnish is lightly put on top. This produces a kind of *crème brûlée* effect, with the still-drying oil-based varnish being the cream, and the water-based varnish being the thin caramel topping. The base varnish moves as it continues drying, and because the dry top coat cannot follow suit, it cracks. The cracking cannot be predicted beyond the general guidelines that the thicker the base varnish the wider the cracks will be, and the thinner the first varnish, the finer the cracks. To speed the effect, you can play a hair dryer across the surface. Once the craquelure is complete, allow it to rest for about an hour. You can then rub colour into the faulted surface to highlight the cracks. The mesh of cracks can aesthetically unite a piece of découpage and, with the help of an antiquing glaze, kindle an otherwise bland project.

Equipment

Oil-based antiquing varnish*
Water-based gum arabic varnish*
Antiquing oil glaze coloured with raw umber
Varnish brushes
Glaze brush
Rags

✱ Further information

Découpage *p.120*
Varnishing *p.29*
Applying mediums *p.16*

1 Apply the oil-based varnish evenly over the area, laying off* in one direction. Remember to have a major light source on the opposite side of the surface so that you can see the glint of the wet varnish and spot any missed patches.

2 When the oil varnish is just dry enough for you to pass the back of your finger over the surface without sticking, apply the water-based cracking varnish evenly over the area. Leave in a warm atmosphere for cracking to develop as drying occurs.

3 Rest the finish for an hour after cracking. Then you can rub an oil-based antiquing glaze into the cracks to give them greater definition. Oil glaze must be used for this because the crackle varnish would react with water and dissolve.

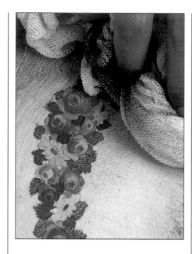

4 Using a circular motion, gently rub the coloured surface with a rag. Change the rag occasionally and continue this procedure until all the excess colour has been removed from the surface. Seal the finish with oil varnish when dry.

Craquelure

Gold stencilling* can often look a little new and brash, even over a black ground. Craquelure gives a wonderful time-worn look to the work and can be extensively used without fear of overplaying the effect. Apply the ground varnish slightly more thickly for this craquelure, and when it is dry enough to touch, coat it liberally with

the second varnish. Drying with a hair dryer will increase the effect and rubbing a tinted glaze, such as the vermilion hue used here, will emphasize the cracks and convey an impression of lacquer. When the work is dry, protect the effect with an oil-based varnish*.

Equipment

*Oil-based antiquing varnish
Water-based gum arabic crackle varnish
Antiquing oil glaze coloured with vermilion hue
Brushes for varnish and glaze
Hair dryer
Rags*

✻ Further information

Stencilling *p.128*
Varnishing *p.29*

2 Let the surface rest for an hour. Rub in the red glaze which will be retained by some of the cracks.

5 The web of craquelure softens the découpage and gives the tray a feeling of age.

1 Lay the water-based gum arabic varnish over a generous coat of oil varnish, which has dried sufficiently to touch. Speed drying with a hair dryer or fan heater. Do not apply the heat too intensely and do not use a naked flame:

these items are combustible and must be treated with care.

3 Wipe off the excess glaze with a rag.

Antiquing paint with craquelure

One antiquing technique is often complemented, enhanced or disguised with another. In this case the initial antiquing effect of rubbing or brushing has been carried out* and craquelure is to be an additional finish. The first finish used a raw umber glaze, and this colour will be employed again in highlighting the cracks.

1 Apply the oil-based varnish, taking extra care with ornate parts where varnish may pool and therefore dry unevenly.

4 The finished effect has softened and aged the gold stencilling.

2 After the allotted time*, apply the coat of water-based varnish.

3 Give the craquelure one hour to dry before rubbing in the raw umber glaze. Remember that the water-based varnish is vulnerable and would dissolve with water, so protect the surface with an oil-based varnish as soon as it is dry.

Equipment

Oil-based antiquing varnish
Water-based gum arabic varnish
Antiquing oil glaze coloured with raw umber
Varnish brushes
Glaze brush
Rags

* Further information

Antiquing (distressing) *p. 43*
Antiquing découpage *p. 37*

Antiquing drag

When the piece to be antiqued needs a direction or grain, antiquing drag is often the answer. This finish, achieved in a similar way to dragging*, is very subtle. The glaze is applied thinly and must be oil-based to ensure the slow drying necessary for a soft, graded result. The ground colour used here is gardenia, and the glaze raw umber. As in standard dragging, the glaze has to move over the surface and therefore preparation* must be of a high quality.

Equipment

Antiquing glaze with raw umber
Glaze brush
*Very fine glasspaper**
Soft-textured rag
Dry paintbrush

❋ Further information

Dragging *p.54*
Preparation *p.17*
Sanding *p.21*

1 Whisk over the surface with a very fine grade of glasspaper to ensure that the finish is smooth and without faults that could collect glaze. Remember to sand with the direction of the drag.

2 Apply the raw umber oil glaze, brushing well out and being careful to penetrate every nook and crevice.

3 Gently wipe the surface backwards and forwards along the line of the drag with a soft-textured rag.

4 Use a dry paintbrush to tease the glaze which has built up at the ends of the panels.

Antiquing handles and fittings

Probably one of the commonest and most unnecessary sights is an antique piece of furniture with bright sparkling handles. Fittings can easily be subdued by applying a coloured glaze, as with woodwork. Boot polish and oak varnish are time-honoured treatments which can work to great effect. As a cabinet collects dust of a particular colour over the years, the fittings are likely to be dirtied with a similar hue. Glaze can unify the overall task and suggest the effects of use as well as conveying a patina of age.

Equipment

Oil-based glaze with raw umber
Glaze brush
Rag
Dry paintbrush

✱ Further information

Stippling *p.104*

1 The pristine knob prior to its treatment. How inappropriate it would look on a piece which had been toned down.

2 Apply the glaze, making sure that it penetrates the details of the design.

3 Wipe the excess glaze from the surface, leaving it in the recesses.

4 Attach the handles, not forgetting to treat the base roses separately. Stipple on* the mixed glaze around the roses, and use the rag and the dry brush to draw the colour away from the handles.

5 The finished effect, suggesting a patina of age where use of the handles over the years has darkened the area around them.

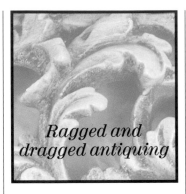

Ragged and dragged antiquing

When an intricate piece is to be antiqued, the effect must be as delicate as possible, so that the changing tone accentuates the play of light and dark and does not distract the attention. In this example a highly detailed cornice is antiqued using ragging* and dragging* techniques combined with raw umber glaze

Equipment

Antiquing glaze tinted with raw umber
Application brush
Dry paintbrush
Lint-free rags

✷ Further information

Ragging *p.88*
Dragging *p.54*
Stippling *p.104*

1 Apply the antiquing glaze, stippling* the areas that are hard to penetrate.

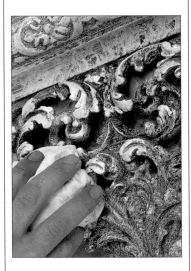

2 Using a soft lint-free rag, pounce over the surface* removing the majority of the glaze from the projecting elements of detail.

3 With the dry paintbrush gently drag* any part of the piece which needs to indicate a direction of movement.

4 The finished effect accentuates the form of this ornate piece.

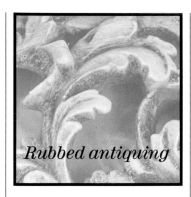

Rubbed antiquing

Although paint effects are normally either applied or subtracted*, rubbed antiquing falls into both categories. It consists of two stages: first the removal of paint, varnish, or another applied effect by wire brushing or sanding; and second, the rubbing of glaze into the surface to suggest grime from years gone by.

Equipment

Antiquing glaze tinted with raw umber
Glaze brush
Wire brush
Coarse-grade sandpaper*
Rag

* Further information

Applied and subtracted
finishes *p.15*
Sanding *p.21*

1 The rather gaudy freshly-painted detail of a chair back.

3 Apply the raw umber glaze over the entire surface. The exposed areas, being more absorbent, will colour more deeply.

2 Brush the surface with the wire brush. Don't be too gentle – the odd prominent scar looks authentic. The surface can be scuffed equally well using coarse sandpaper.

4 Rub the surface with the rag, allowing the glaze to remain in the hollows and niches of the piece.

Antiquing stipple

The aim of this effect is to reproduce that patina of age on pieces of furniture shown by a gradation of colour from dark to light – like the ivory keys on an old piano whose pale centres darken as they near the neighbouring keys. So the first step is to establish where the piece would be pale and where dark. For example, the majority of erosion on a table occurs in the middle, because it is easy to clean and because heavier items tend to be positioned there. If, however, the table has a large lamp at its centre and this was rarely moved, the colour grading is likely to be reversed. Like most skills, antiquing needs practice, but you can learn an enormous amount by examining old pieces to see how and where such lighter and darker areas occur.

The fine texture of stipple which lends itself especially well to the even application of glaze, makes it ideal for this kind of antiquing. The technique most often used is blended or tonal stippling*. Oil mediums are best, and you will need two glazes of a standard antiquing earth colour*, such as raw umber – one a stronger tone than the other. Wipe the surface over with a slightly thinned untinted oil glaze to help the colours move. Then apply the paler glaze, around the outside or in the centre, whichever is appropriate. The darker medium comes next, so you need only one application brush. Next, stipple the darker tone into the lighter, remembering to clean the brush before returning to the dark patch. The effect is very delicate and is best appreciated from a distance. Often it is complemented with a spatter*, or water-stained – or both.

Equipment

Untinted oil glaze thinned with white spirit
Antiquing glaze tinted mediumly with raw umber
Antiquing glaze tinted darkly with raw umber
Application brush
Decorator's dusting brush
Rag

✻ Further information

Stippling *p.104*
Antiquing colours *p.36*
Spattering *p.96*
Water-staining *p.45*

1 Wipe the surface with the thinned untinted glaze and then apply the paler of the two tinted glazes, leaving clear the area which is to be darker.

3 Using the decorator's dusting brush, stipple from dark to light, remembering to rub the brush clean with a rag each time before returning to the surface.

2 Apply the darker glaze.

4 The finished effect shows the subtle colour gradient to perfection.

Water-staining

1 Spatter the freshly worked oil-based glaze with methylated spirit.

Like fleck spatter, this is a complementary finish, normally associated with antique stipple*. The effect is achieved by spattering* methylated spirits over an oil-based glaze.

Equipment

Methylated spirit
Oil-based antiquing glaze
Spatter brush*

* Further information

Antiquing stipple *p.44*
Spattering *p.96*
Brushes *p.24*

2 Pale rings appear which resemble water damage.

Antiquing fleck spatter

1 Using the fitch, spatter the surface with glaze.

This effect is generally used over a drag*, or where a direction has been indicated. In graining* it is often used instead of a check roller* to imitate the pores of the wood. The effect is obtained by softly brushing over spatter* while it is still wet, and is therefore best achieved with an oil glaze.

Equipment

Antiquing oil glaze tinted with raw umber
Fitch*
Dry paintbrush

* Further information

Dragging *p.54*
Graining *p.63*
Check rolling *p.46*
Spattering *p.96*
Brushes *p.24*

2 Gently soften the spots of glaze in the direction of the ground coat drag.

Check rolling

This effect, which resembles the pores found in oak and other woods, is a complementary finish, used with dragging, wood-graining and flogging. It is achieved with a 5 cm (2 in) hog-hair mottler* and a specially designed check or tick roller*. This combination of tools is primarily used in graining*, but produces a delightful effect in its own right. It is also known as tick rolling.

Oil- or water-based glaze* can be used. But the slower drying time of oil gives you the opportunity to soften or smudge the effect while it is still wet.

✱ Further information
Brushes/Equipment *p.22*
Graining *p.63*
Mediums *p.10*

Equipment
Check or tick roller
Hog-hair mottler
Paint or glaze
Softening brush

1 Load the hog-hair mottler with glaze and clasp it with your thumb to the top of the roller. The bristles should feed the revolving discs of the roller as you push it along.

2 Make sure that the tracks remain roughly parallel and travel in the direction of the grain.

3 You can use a softening brush* to smooth the effect while the glaze is still wet.

4 The finished effect looks smartly formal (especially when a pale top coat is used over a dark ground) when applied to boxes or occasional furniture.

Colour washing

Many experts refer with fondness to the old-style distemper (made from water and pigment bound with casein, egg or glue) that was originally used to produce this finish. However, although it was cheap and produced quick results, it did not cover or wear well. Modern decorators use either water-based or oil-based glazes to achieve this effect. The techniques are the same for both, apart from their drying times, but as this is an applied effect*, the water-based medium is recommended.

Colour wash on wood

You can colour wash wood with thinned-down emulsion* or latex*, which is slightly opaque, or use a true transparent wash, consisting of pure colour –

2 Allow to dry. The brush marks, which are clearly apparent, criss-cross unevenly over the surface.

3 Using the same glaze and brush, apply the second coat. Try to make the brush strokes cross those underneath.

Walls

1 Apply the glaze lightly with a standard decorating brush*. Vary the angle and direction of the brush, allowing the ground to show through.

4 The completed effect is an undulating finish with a refreshing crispness.

Equipment

Paint or glaze
Brush
2 cloths (1 damp)

watercolour, gouache, or a powder – suspended in water*. But you need to take certain precautions first.

When raw wood is dampened with a water-based medium, its sponge-like reactions lead to the rising of the grain. If you want a soft effect, it is wise to dampen down the surface of the wood first with a clean, damp cloth. When the wood is dry, flatten the raised grain with a fine abrasive paper* and block* before proceeding.

If you are colour washing a piece of furniture that has been stripped to its raw state, neutralize the surface by washing it down with a mixture of one part vinegar to twenty parts water.

A piece made from raw new timber needs to be checked for any filled areas. These will not be porous, and will therefore refuse to take the colour. You can touch in small, unobtrusive fillings with colour later. But if the filling is extensive, you may have to consider a different effect.

* Further information

Applied and subtracted
finishes *p.15*
Brushes/Equipment *p.22*
Mediums *p.10*
Sanding *p.21*

Wood
1 Apply the thinned colour quickly to cover the area without patches.

2 Rub over the surface with an absorbent cloth to remove the excess wash.

3 Use a damp cloth to clean up any remaining surface colour.

Combing

Basketwork
combing
◆
Weave combing
◆
Watered silk
◆
Moiré

There are endless possibilities for this simple finish, which is often seen in large scale on floors. Different combs and handling techniques can produce a multitude of effects ranging from the primitive to the luxurious. Combing was popular in the 1920s and 1930s, when it appeared in dull, sombre colours. The combs were made of metal, card and wood, and were drawn over the surface of wet paint to produce a constrasting textured effect. The combs had been developed far earlier for the more refined process of graining*, but by the beginning of the 20th century graining had gone out of fashion.

Combing can be tackled with water- or oil-based glaze. In fact, if the area is small enough, normal undercoat or emulsion can be used. Allow this to begin tacking off before you start combing; otherwise the paint will flow back into the marks made by the comb. If you use home-made combs* (see page 27), don't let the top coat get too tacky, or the card may not be strong enough to force its way through. Rubber, leather and steel combs are available through specialist shops.

Basketwork combing

This technique is primarily a floor application, but can be extremely effective on a smaller scale. Suited to subtle colours, such as soft greys and pale blues or yellows, the design can be applied in a chessboard pattern, or at a 45° angle for more of a basketwork effect.

Equipment
Paint or glaze
Brush
Comb
Rag

✱ Further information
Graining *p.63*
Equipment *p.22*

1 Apply the glaze.

2 Drag the comb (in this case a steel one) through the glaze, angling it slightly towards you. The drag should be roughly the same length as the width of the comb.

3 Comb at 90° to the first imprint, again angling the comb to produce a square imprint the same size as the first one.

4 Continue to produce the repeated alternating print, remembering to keep the comb clean by wiping with a rag from time to time.

5 The finished effect. Some of the comb marks are bound to be a little skewed. This gives a softness and slight movement which adds to the effect.

Weave

You can create a weave or plaid effect by introducing a second or even a third colour, strategically applied over a wet ground coat. Combs of different grades and widths, dragged across the surface at right angles to each other, help enhance this effect.

Equipment
2 paints or glazes
2 brushes
2 combs (10cm/4in fine and 25cm/11in coarse)

✱ Further information
Applying mediums *p.16*

1 Apply the ground colour and lay off*. Using a clean brush, paint on a further colour in stripes. The brush of the second colour will need to be well loaded as the ground is still wet.

2 Pull a 10cm (4in) wide fine-grade comb across the surface, along the lines of the second colour.

3 Using a 25mm (1in) coarse-grade comb, drag equidistant strips across your first marks, about 5cm (2in) apart. The final effect has the appearance of a subtle, rich weave or a plaid.

Watered silk

This effect is much more luxurious than most combing techniques and is produced here using a triangular rubber comb. Steel combs will create a finer and more delicate look.

Equipment
Paint or glaze
Brush
Comb

✴ Further information
Applying mediums *p.16*

1 Apply the glaze and lay off* in the direction in which the effect will run.

2 Pull the comb through the glaze in a straight line, but smoothly change the angle of the comb, so as to produce an alternately broadening and narrowing stripe.

4 When the area is completed and while the glaze is still wet, pull the comb in a straight line through the pattern. As if by magic, a watered silk effect appears.

Moiré

This effect is a close cousin to that of watered silk. However, it is far less flowing and more mechanical. Patterns like the one shown here can be so pronounced that they produce an illusion of movement. This harsh colour contrast has been chosen to demonstrate the optical effect of moiré and subtler combinations would normally be used.

Equipment
Paint or glaze
Brush
Comb

❋ Further information
Applying mediums *p.16*

3 Create a second swirling stripe to fit snugly alongside the first. Each succeeding stripe should complement the one before: broad where the preceeding one was narrow, and narrow where it was broad.

5 The finished effect, with its rings of watered silk, is particularly effective on small items or when combined with an antique finish.

1 Apply the glaze and lay off* in the direction of the combing.

3 Cover the area using the same technique, filling in the undulations and maintaining the rhythm of the previous strip. Do not change the angle of the comb.

4 Drag the comb in a straight line through the pattern while the glaze is still wet. As with watered silk, the moiré will magically come to life.

2 Pull the comb through the glaze, curving from side to side but keeping the face of the comb pointing directly towards you.

5 The finished effect is brash and would be difficult to look at for long periods. However, if you use pale colours with less contrast between base and top coats the finished effect can be very attractive.

Dragging

Dragging walls
◆
Dragging wood

Dragging walls

Dragging is an underrated effect and easy to execute providing it is well planned. As the name implies, the technique involves dragging a brush through an applied glaze coat, and it leaves fine brush marks where the ground smiles through. Because the top coat is pulled across the surface, high-quality preparation is important. All dents, lines and nibs must have been filled or removed before the glaze coat is applied, as these would otherwise catch the colour and be high-lighted, thereby marring the effect. Just prior to top coating, check that the surface is smooth by lightly wisping over it with a 320 grit paper*, remembering to move in the direction of the drag.

When choosing colours, bear in mind that this effect first became popular in the 1930s, thanks largely to designer John Fowler, whose work of the period in English country houses is renowned. The colours were reserved, and often very subtle indeed. The base colour would be tinted towards the glaze coat colour to make only the slightest contrast between the two. Although strong colours have been used with great success, this effect usually benefits from delicate colour. The finest examples of dragging on walls occur when its presence is hardly noticeable but it lends the room an air of quality and elegance.

Dragging is a subtracted finish*, and when the effect is to be achieved on a large area, a time-efficient technique must be employed. Oil-based glazes are normally used, but on small surfaces emulsion-based glazes can give good results. Water-based drag will be matt, whereas oil-based drag dries to a sheen. The brush to use depends on the area which requires finishing. Walls need either a 15 cm (6 in) flogger*, a 22.5 cm (9 in) dragger*, or a doctored emulsion brush. Floggers and draggers are graining brushes with long bristles, which pick up glaze easily when pulled across the surface. You can doctor an emulsion brush by cutting a line of bristles to thin them out. This will give the brush a better marking quality.

Glaze is normally applied by brush, but you can use a roller on walls. When using a brush apply the glaze thinly and evenly and lay off* in the direction of the proposed drag. The first dragging stroke will be guided by the adjacent wall. Subsequent strokes, which should be parallel to this, will be unguided and consequently more challenging for the inexperienced. Try to maintain a relaxed wrist and allow the brush to do the work. Hold the brush at an angle of approximately 30° to the surface and pull downwards through the glaze. Where the situation allows, you might find it helpful to use a giant ruler made from a straight edge of timber with nails hammered through to keep it clear of the surface. But hand dragging is preferable. It is far quicker, and minor wiggles and deviations will not be as obvious as you might think. Remember to keep the dragging brush clean by wiping it occasionally with a rag. Turning the brush over to utilize both faces can also be helpful.

The commonest problems when dragging walls are twofold. The first, known as curtaining, appears at the top of the wall where the dragging brush takes a grip of the glaze. If the glaze is applied too thickly this effect will be unattractive, and the glaze will need to be teased downwards with a dry paintbrush. The second problem also results from the amount of glaze applied. The bottom of the wall, where the dragging stroke finishes, will tend to be heavy with glaze. To combat this, pressure on the bristles should be lessened slightly so that less glaze is picked up by the brush on the lower part of the wall. Alternatively, the brush can be dragged in a flicking stroke back up the wall. This must be done with great care, and each stroke should end at a different point so as to stagger, and therefore blend, the effect with the rest of the wall.

If the wall is high enough to need a ladder, you will have to interrupt the dragging stroke to make your descent. The brush must not be stopped while in contact with the surface. The travel must continue as the brush is lifted away. When you continue the drag, your stroke must begin its movement before the brush makes contact with the surface. The more smoothly you carry out these two operations, the less obvious the joins will be. It is wise to alternate the point on the wall where these breaks occur to make them less apparent.

Equipment

Paintbrush and/or roller
Paint or glaze
Dragger or flogger (15cm/6in or 22.5cm/9in)
Rags

✱ Further information

Sanding/abrasive paper
chart *p.21*
Applied and subtractive
finishes *p.15*
Brushes/Equipment *p.22*
Applying mediums *p.16*
Painting order *p.16*

1 Apply the glaze thinly and evenly, ensuring that it is laid off in the direction of the intended drag.

2 Drag the brush smoothly through the glaze, allowing the bristles to do the work. Hold the brush at an angle of about 30° to the surface.

3 Wipe the dragging brush regularly with a rag to keep it unclogged and therefore able to produce the same effect across the surface.

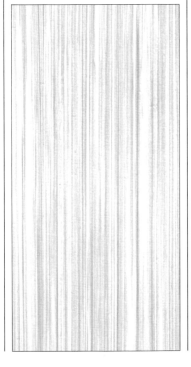

4 The finished effect. The joins should be almost imperceptible.

Dragging wood

Dragging has its origins in graining, and when dragging woodwork similarities of technique remain. The size of brush will depend on the piece that is to be dragged. For a large table-top, a large brush will make the operation much easier. In general, however, woodwork finishing requires a smaller brush: a 7.5 cm (3 in) flogger* or a 3.75–5 cm (1½–2 in) dragger* would be ideal.

Woodwork must be dragged with the grain or, if particle board is used, the way the grain would run. If there is a choice of direction, always drag the length of the panel. The most important aspect of dragging woodwork is the order in which the piece is tackled. If a standard panel door is to be dragged, each section should be dealt with individually. If need be, you can mask each section off and allow it to dry before working on the next. When you become more proficient, you will be able to complete the entire door without stopping. But it is essential to apply glaze and drag the confined pieces of wood first in order to achieve a clean joint line*. The joints can be emphasized with a fine line when the glaze is dry to give extra sharpness.

Equipment
Paint or glaze
Paintbrush
Flogger (7.5cm/3in or 3.75–5cm/1½–2in)
Rags

2 Apply the glaze to the rail* and drag. Note that the drag begins before the joint line. Complete the second rail in the same way.

1 Apply the glaze and drag the panel, first ensuring that you lay off in the direction of the drag. If the panel is square, the drag is normally vertical. Wipe clean the surrounding area.

3 Apply the glaze to the stile*, carefully rubbing glaze up to the joint.

4 Drag the brush through the glaze. The dragging stroke should begin with the bristles overlapping the edge of the stile, so as to avoid a curtaining effect. The finished texture is very subtle, giving an impression of opulence.

Faux bamboo

Equipment

Dowel
Plaster of Paris
Fine grade glasspaper
Craft knife
Pale yellow base coat
Raw umber glaze
Round brush
Artist's 0 or 00 brush

Bamboo has always been a popular material for the construction of buildings and furniture in the East. Its combined assets of lightness and strength have ensured its constant use up to the present day. Furniture made from this giant tropical grass was introduced to Europe during the 17th century due to increased trade with China and became highly fashionable. But the expense of bringing furniture from the Far East precluded many from owning it. So European craftworkers quickly began making and painting pieces of furniture to look as if they were constructed from bamboo. The fashion reached its peak in the 18th century, when the production of faux, or simulated, bamboo expanded to fantasy effects in brilliant colours.

To make faux bamboo, begin with a length of dowel. As bamboo varies in diameter, any size of dowel will do. Build up the "joints" with plaster of Paris, and smooth them down ready for paint. The ground colour is a pale yellow, and the glaze coat a raw umber. Protect the finished piece with two coats of matt varnish and then polish with a clear wax.*

❋ Further information

Sanding/Abrasive paper chart *p.21*
Applying mediums *p.16*
Finishing *p.31*

1 Slightly dampen the dowel before rolling on the plaster of Paris with a finger.

2 When the application is dry, sand it with a fine grade of abrasive paper*, carefully shaping the joint. Using a craft knife, gently incise a groove around the middle of the joint.

3 Apply the base coat of pale yellow, and lay off* the paint lengthwise.

4 When the ground coat is dry, sand with a fine-grade paper. Apply the raw umber glaze coat and lightly drag it along the stem.

6 The finished effect. Faux bamboo can be used instead of real bamboo (if this is unavailable) for furniture, staircases or picture frames.

5 Again using the raw umber glaze, paint on the joint groove, the spine and the eyes.

Faux stone blocks

Equipment

Finishing plaster
Water
Heavy-duty bucket
Broom handle or other
mixing stick
Spot board*
Hawk*
Laying-on trowel*
Bucket with water
Old emulsion brush
Plumb-line
Spirit-level
Straight-edge
Measuring tape
Trowel

Faux stone blocks became fashionable in the 18th century, when the art of marbling* was extended to include granite and sandstone. The effect was popular because it lent an air of strength and durability to an interior, and was also much easier to achieve than marbling. Spattering* and sponging* were used to simulate texture, and the blocks were defined by a simple *trompe-l'oeil** line.

The technique of faux stone blocks is partly borrowed from stucco work which was often treated with a block-like effect. Stucco is a quick-setting plaster with an added strengthener such as ground marble. Stucco work dates back to antiquity, but gained popularity in the 16th century in Italy, from where it spread throughout Europe. The architect Inigo Jones is thought to have been the first to promote stucco in England when he used it in conjunction with Portland stone dressings on the Queen's House at Greenwich (1616-35) and the Queen's Chapel in London (1623-27). Faux stone blocks increasingly became an interior feature, and by the latter part of the 18th century the fashion had spread to North America, where some fine examples can be found in the hallways and reception rooms of Empire-style houses.

Creating stone-blocks

A simple stone-block effect can be produced by marking out the selected wall area with a plumb-line and spirit-level, and sponging and spattering the surface, which is then divided into blocks by painted lines. This is an effective way of achieving a sober, elegant look. The example shown combines the paint technique with a stucco-like texture, and would be suitable when a more rustic effect is required. The surface must be plastered to help create the texture. There is no need to be put off by this. It is true that plastering cannot be learned in a matter of hours and specialists may take years to bring their skills to perfection, but the textured technique used here cuts out the real difficulty of plastering, and that of smoothing off.

Prepare your wall in the same way as for any other effect*, but add an unthinned coat of PVA adhesive, and allow to dry. You will need finishing plaster for this technique because it can be used thicker than normal plasters and also offers a longer drying time in which to complete the effect. An all-purpose DIY finishing plaster has been used in the example here, but it is worth seeking out specialist finishing plaster to achieve successful texturing. Do not buy the plaster until your preparation is complete. Plaster goes stale, and must be used fresh. Most bags of plaster are date-stamped, and need to be used within six weeks of the date. Always keep the bag in a dry place. If any water comes into contact with the plaster before use, it will almost certainly be spoiled. Plastering can be very messy, especially if you have never done it before, so it is advisable to clear the room of furnishings and dust-sheet everything that's left. The plaster dust will hang in the air and could scratch polished surfaces even hours later. Heavy-duty bin liners are essential later for dropped or old plaster.

Mixing plaster

When mixing plaster use only fresh water, as impurities in rainwater or buttwater may be detrimental to the plaster. Mix the plaster in a heavy-duty plastic bucket, a little at a time. Mixing is the most tiring part of plastering, and the more mixture in the bucket, the harder the task. A third of a bucket is probably the most that should be attempted at one time. Put the water in first; otherwise the plaster will clog and stick to the side of the bucket. Stir continuously as you add the powdered plaster to the water, using a strong stick, such as a broom handle. Continue stirring until all the powder is incorporated, and when the consistency is stiff enough to support the mixing stick but still workable, pour the plaster onto the spot board. Clean the bucket and stick immediately with water, or any remaining plaster will harden and be difficult to remove. The cleanliness of tools is one of the most important and under-recognized keys to success in plastering.

Applying the plaster

Plastering is a homely procedure without mystique. The same basic tools have been doing the job successfully for countless years, and the task itself is not unlike icing a gigantic cake.

Use an old emulsion brush and a bucket of water to dampen all the tools before use. Quickly dampen the wall also to retard the plaster's drying time. Hold the hawk in your left hand if you are right-handed – the reverse for left-handers – and position it just under the edge of the spot board, so that you can scrape a portion of plaster onto it with the laying-on trowel. The amount should be just enough to support comfortably on the trowel. The action of loading the hawk should be like scooping crumbs from a table onto your hand.

Approach the wall as if you were going to paint it – probably from left to right, if you are right-handed and vice versa if left handed. Offer up the loaded hawk so that its edge is in contact with the wall. Unlike painting, you should begin by pushing in an upward arc from a point just above the skirting. Once you have got the plaster on the wall in swirls, you can smooth it out and stretch it over a much greater area. Do this with a clean trowel, freshly washed with a brush and water from the nearby bucket.

Spread the plaster with the trowel as if you were spreading butter. Angle the trowel like the knife so as to allow the correct amount of plaster to be squeezed under the blade. If the angle is too small, the plaster will slip under the trowel and remain in a lump. If the angle is too great, the trowel will scrape the plaster so that it breaks, and the plaster on the trowel will probably become dislodged and fall off. Try to avoid this scraping which is similar to scraping a minimum of butter onto toast. Discard any plaster which has been allowed to fall to the floor. When the wall is covered and spread to a thickness of approximately 5 mm (³⁄₁₆ in), you will be ready to apply the texturing.

Texturing

The finishing plaster used in this example allows an hour's finishing time to complete the texturing. Begin by marking off the chosen depth of block from an adjacent wall. Then use the straight-edge in conjunction with the spirit-level to work your way across the surface, laying the straight-edge onto the wet plaster. With these horizontal lines completed, you can mark the staggered vertical ones with the aid of the plumb-line and trowel. You can then texture the faces of the outlined alternating blocks using all manner of implements. Sponges* give an excellent effect. A coarser texture, as in this example, is achieved with an Artex stippler* and then smoothed over with a trowel. Whatever method you use, it is important to treat the blocks as separate entities.

1 Complete the final stage of the texturing coat, using the laying-on trowel to smooth the surface. Leave to dry overnight.

Equipment

Raw sienna wash and application brush
White emulsion* and application brush
Pale grey emulsion
Sword brush*
PVA sealer
Rags*

* Further information

Marbling *p.75*
Spattering *p.96*
Sponging *p.98*
Trompe-l'oeil p.136
Preparation *p.17*
Equipment *p.22*
Plastering tools *p.28*
Coarse stippling *p.106*
Washes *p.12*
Mediums *p.10*

2 Thin the raw sienna colour with water, and apply it liberally with a brush. Work small sections at a time, as the plaster is very porous and will soak up the wash rapidly.

3 Rub on water-thinned white emulsion, covering the area which has been treated with sienna.

5 Paint in pale grey mortar lines with the sword brush.

4 Rub each block with a rag so that in some areas the sienna colour fills the depressions and in others covers the white. Continue colouring sections with the sienna and white application and rubbing with the rag until the entire area is treated.

6 When the surface is dry, protect it with a water-based sealer, such as PVA.

Flogging

Like dragging, flogging is a technique used in graining, and has only recently become an effect in its own right. More often seen on walls than on woodwork or furniture, this finish is usually most successful in subtle colours, but can look stunning in strong yellows, perhaps because of its resemblance to a cornfield. The effect is achieved in a subtracted manner*, and flogging refers to the action of slapping the brush against the wet glaze.

The glaze is applied with a brush or roller and laid off* in the same direction as the flog. Unlike dragging, the effect is initiated at the bottom of the wall, and the work progresses upwards. A flogger or dragger is the only suitable brush, as long bristles are essential to the effect. As the brush slaps the glaze, it is also pushed across the surface, causing the outer bristles to splay slightly. The glaze does not have to be pulled over the surface, so providing the preparation is reasonable, the finish will be successful. Keep wiping the brush with a rag to maintain a uniform overall effect.

Equipment

Paintbrush or roller
Paint or glaze
Flogger or dragger
Rags

* Further information

Applied and subtractive
finishes *p.15*
Applying mediums *p.16*

1 Apply the glaze, using either roller or brush, and lay off in the direction of the flog.

2 Start at the bottom of the area. Slap the glaze with the flogger, and at the same time move the brush in an upwards direction over the surface.

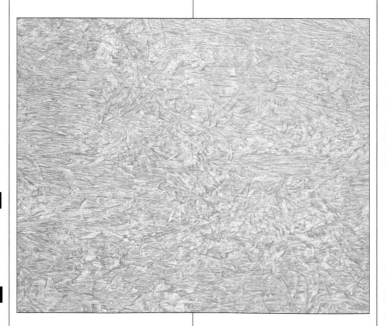

3 The completed effect has a more homey feel than that produced by dragging.

Graining

Clair bois

◆

Bird's-eye maple

◆

Mahogany

◆

Graining by roller

Graining is thought to date back to ancient Egypt where a shortage of wood stimulated the development of techniques to imitate wood grain. Similar faux, or imitation, wood finishes later emerged in Europe in response to demands for hard-to-obtain or exotic woods.

Although there are earlier examples, graining appears to have become popular in England in the latter part of the 17th century, possibly as an indirect consequence of the Great Fire of London in 1666. The oak needed to rebuild the city depleted stocks to such an extent that fixtures had to be wrought from pine. This cheaper wood was disguised by graining.

In reality, however, the fire was probably only one among many contributory factors. The age of oak was nearing its end, and more decorative walnut furniture was in the ascendency. In panelling too, oak was gradually supplanted by lime or pine, painted in a shade of yellowish-brown known as drab green, or grained.

It is difficult to ascertain just how widely graining was used, because, by its very nature, it was likely to be removed and redecorated with the passing of time. Quality improved, however, and by the 1850s an extremely high standard of work was being produced. Unfortunately this did not prevent graining from acquiring a bad reputation by the 1930s, when the most basic of techniques was employed together with a thick tar-like glaze which rendered surfaces anything but attractive.

Graining today

Today, techniques have again become highly sophisticated and capable of producing effects that are indistinguishable from the original. Some of these are very complex, but you can achieve effective finishes more simply (and it is advisable to stick to these in the early stages). Once you have mastered the basic graining techniques, you may decide to move on to more complicated variations.

The three types of graining shown here are an introductory effect called *clair bois* (meaning pale wood), a mahogany effect suitable for large areas such as doors and furniture, and a bird's-eye maple for small pieces like boxes or mirrors. All the techniques have been simplified as much as possible to give an attractive effect with the least amount of effort.

As with most faux finishes, a feeling of depth is achieved by layering the different colours. In most cases the medium is transparent oil glaze, sometimes in combination with a wash. The ground colour should be a shade lighter than the palest part of the wood being copied, and the graining colour, or top coat, should be a shade darker than the darkest part.

Clair bois

This pale wood graining effect is easy to achieve and can be extremely effective, especially when used in conjunction with black borders or lines, which will give a late French Empire or Biedermeier look to a piece.

Equipment
Raw sienna oil glaze mix
Application brush
Flogger
Rags

✱ Further information
Mixing glazes *p.13*
Mediums *p.10*
Flogger *p.24*
Applying mediums *p.16*

1 Brush on the oil glaze mixture, and lay off* in the direction in which the grain will run.

2 Use the flogger to pat the glaze in such a way that almost the entire length of the bristles is in contact with the surface. Work away from your body, lifting the flogger off the work before patting.

3 The finished effect closely simulates a pale wood.

Bird's-eye maple

The use of grained softwoods gained momentum in Europe at the time of the French Revolution, when harder wood was increasingly channelled toward military purposes. Locally grown beech and pine, or deal, were readily available but interest turned to more exotic woods in the desire for new effects. Bird's-eye maple was one example which grew in popularity until the mid-19th century, when graining was sneered at by the pundits of the day and went into decline.

Used in the past for large areas, such as panelling, a bird's-eye maple effect is extremely attractive for small oddments, such as boxes or mirror frames. The medium in this example is water-based, which gives a cleaner and finer finish. It is applied over a pale honey oil-based ground, and in order to allow the water-based wash to spread freely over the surface, all surface oil must be removed. Prepare the ground by rubbing it over with whiting*, using a rag or pounce bag*. Mix the wash* from powder colour and water, using a 2:1 blend of raw sienna and raw umber. Apply the wash, laying off* in the direction of the grain, and treat using a hog-hair mottler* in an action which combines dragging and walking the brush over the surface. Continue this in parallel bands until the surface is covered. Using a dampened fingertip, touch the wet surface to make a bird's-eye print. Repeat the marks in small groups over the entire area. Try to avoid making the prints too contrived or you may get a polka-dot effect. Use a badger brush* to soften the effect in all directions before allowing it to dry, when it should be varnished.

Equipment

Whiting
Wash of raw sienna and raw umber mixed 2:1
Application brush
Hog-hair mottler
Badger-hair softener
Rag or pounce bag

✱ Further information

Whiting *p.20*
Pounce bag *p.28*
Mixing washes *p.13*
Laying off *p.16*
Brushes *p.24*

1 Rub over the oil-based ground coat with whiting, using a pounce bag or rag.

2 Apply the raw sienna/raw umber mix, and lay off* in the direction of the grain.

4 Dampen the tip of your finger and touch the wet wash to create the bird's-eye marks. These should be scattered over the area randomly but in vague groupings.

3 Drag a hog-hair mottler across the surface, moving one edge of the brush slightly in front of the other, and then the reverse, in an action like walking.

5 Soften the entire surface using a badger brush in all directions. This brush is so soft that it barely supports the weight of its stock. It should be used so delicately that the tips of the bristles barely touch the surface during the stroke, and it will gently blur the wash into a softer effect.

6 The pattern should not look repetitive. It helps to have a picture of the real wood as a visual reference while you work.

Mahogany

This finely figured wood was first used by Europeans to repair their ships while exploring the West Indies. One of its earliest documented uses in England was at Nottingham Castle in 1680, but over the next 50 years it became so popular that regular shipments from Central America could no longer meet demand, and a further supplier had to be found. Mahogany began to be imported from Africa as well, and fine veneers were glued onto deal carcases so as to reduce the cost.

The graining of this wood is more complicated than the two earlier examples. As with many graining techniques, there is more than one application. The undergrain is allowed to dry before first a figuring glaze and then the overgrain are applied on top. The undergrain is often oil-based, and the overgrain water-based to give a finer finish, but it is easier to practise the method with one medium at first, and in this example oil-based glazes are used throughout. The ground colour for mahogany should be a brownish terracotta hue, but an exact match is not necessary. The colour of a piece of wood depends on many factors, and it would be impossible to dictate a colour that reflects all the individual variations found in nature.

Equipment

Undergrain glaze (one part raw umber, one part raw sienna, one part Vandyke brown)
Figuring glaze (one part burnt umber, one part Vandyke brown)
Overgrain glaze (burnt umber)
Application brushes for glazes
Hog-hair mottler
Badger-hair softener
Flogger
Cotton rag

✱ Further information

Mediums *p.10*
Mixing glazes *p.13*
Brushes *p.24*
Flogging *p.62*
Laying off *p.16*
Dragging *p.54*
Clair bois *p.63*

1 "Rub on" the thin undergrain glaze with the application brush. Lay off* in the direction of the grain.

2 Using the mottler*, drag* with the proposed grain to produce even colouring and a faint drag.

3 Continue with the mottler, this time used at a 90° angle to the previous strokes. Maintain this attitude as you etch in the annular rings, starting at the bottom with the smaller ring and building up. In this way, the bands get larger as they reach the summit of the figure and reduce as they fall level with the centre.

4 Once you have put in the main figure, gently drag in the remainder of the panel with the mottler returned to its original attitude. A slight movement of the hand similar to the technique used in bird's-eye maple will feather the edge. Leave to dry.

7 Apply the overgrain glaze, laying it off in the direction of the grain.

9 The finished effect relies for its success on the pattern, depth of colour and smooth surface.

5 Using the hog-hair mottler and the figuring glaze, repeat the technique in step **3**. However, in this case the glaze is being applied instead of being removed.

6 Soften the figuring from the centre outwards with the badger-hair brush and allow to dry.

8 Flog* the panel with the flogging brush, working from the bottom upwards, using a similar technique to that for clair bois*. Once dry, the panel should be varnished.

Graining by roller

Graining rollers offer a quick method of achieving a wood-like effect with a minimum of effort. Professional grainers are likely to pale at the thought of using them, because they need so little skill. There are many different sizes and grades of roller on the market. They can be used with oil- or water-based glazes but oil is the best choice for large areas, because it stays "live" longer, giving you more time to complete the technique. A soft colour would be the most suitable counterpoint for the rough-hewn texture of this effect.

The term "roller" is slightly misleading, a key part of the action needed to use this device is more like rocking. This movement is made while you pull the roller across the surface. You will need to wipe the roller clean from time to time to prevent it from clogging with glaze.

1 Apply the glaze with a brush or roller, and lay off* in the direction of the grain.

2 The open edge of the graining roller must be the leading edge when pulling through the glaze.

Equipment

Paint or glaze
Brush or roller
Graining roller
Rags

＊ Further information

Applying mediums *p.16*
Combing: watered silk *p.51*

3 Hold the roller between fingers and thumb and drag it across the surface, rocking it gently at the same time. The rocking motion should be like turning a key in a lock. When beginning your drag, lean the roller so that the open edge is in contact with the surface. As you perfect the technique, keeping the roller at a constant angle, you can alter the attitude to its direction to achieve an undulating pattern, as in watered silk*.

Lapis lazuli

Equipment
Ultramarine glaze and brush
Prussian blue glaze and brush
Bronze powder
White spirit
Lint-free cotton rag
Sword brush
Artist's round brush

A beautiful deep blue opaque stone with gold flecks, once dubbed "the heaven stone", lapis lazuli has always been valued highly. Originally found in Iran and Russia, it was ground down to create ultramarine blue. Highly expensive, ultramarine embellished many rich medieval paintings, where it was associated with purity and goodness. The Virgin Mary was nearly always depicted in this colour. Today ultramarine is made from other pigments, and the only remaining supplies of lapis lazuli, from Chile and Afghanistan, lack the quality of depth and the number of gold flecks (iron pyrites) that were so distinctive in the earlier stones.

The following effect is a suggestive finish rather than an exact facsimile of lapis lazuli. In nature the gold would be less prevalent, and the veining less pronounced. However, this finish looks very effective on table insets, boxes and lamp bases. You should apply a blue-grey ground in readiness for the effect, but as with any faux finish, such as marbling* or graining*, there can be no absolute colour dictates, because natural substances vary among themselves.

The surface should be horizontal when the finish is applied. You can use a water- or oil-based medium* but, as always, the oil-based technique is easier to work because of its slower drying time, and it also tends to give a deeper effect. Mix the medium with a high ratio of colour to reduce the yellowing of the glaze*. Apply ultramarine glaze first, and rag it over with a loosely crushed lint-free cotton rag*. While the ragged surface is still wet, paint on Prussian blue tinted glaze, in patches. Rag this in the same way as the first glaze, and then etch veins into the wet ground with a sword brush* fully loaded with white spirit. Pick up some bronze powder* on an artist's round brush* and add it to the veins. Use a larger brush to repeat the process adding gold or bronze powder especially where the blue is darkest. When the surface is completely dry, seal it with an emulsion glaze, and smooth it with wet-and-dry paper*, after which it can be finished with extra pale varnish* or emulsion glaze.

✸ Further information
Marbling *p.75*
Graining *p.63*
Mediums *p.10*
Yellowing of glazes *p.13*
Ragging *p.88*
Brushes *p.24*
Bronze and gold powder *p.28*
Abrasive papers *p.21*
Varnishing *p.29*
Laying off *p.16*

1 Apply the ultramarine glaze with a brush. The surface should be well covered and the glaze not laid off*.

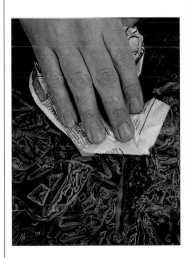

2 Break up the wet glaze by ragging with newspaper or paper, crushed into an open pad. Keep using the same part of the paper: the object of this technique is to displace the glaze rather than absorb it.

3 Apply the Prussian blue glaze strategically to give an undulating appearance.

5 Load the sword brush with white spirit, and burn through the still wet glaze to create veins that meander and fracture.

7 White spirit can be spattered onto the darker patches to produce a more even effect.

8 Picking up just bronze powder on the dampened sword brush, highlight the places where the veins meet.

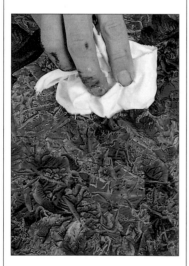

4 Using a cotton rag, break these areas up by ragging as before.

6 Use an artist's round brush, loaded with white spirit and bronze powder, to wander wider, gold-bearing veins through the ground.

9 When the surface is completely dry (which could take several days) protect the finish by sealing, then varnishing or waxing.

Liming

Liming is a very similar effect to pickling*, but originates from a much earlier technique. Liming dates back to 16th-century Europe, when an unction containing the very corrosive slaked lime was applied to furniture and panelling to prevent worm and beetle infestation. Trapped in the pores of the open-grained timber, such as oak and elm, that was most widely used at the time the white paste not only repelled the pests but also produced a pleasing visual effect. This became increasingly popular reaching its height in the 17th century.

Open-grained wood is still the best for this effect, and you will only need to give it a light brushing with a wire brush* prior to treatment. Close-grained woods will need more work with the brush. Once the grain has been readied in this way, you can apply a liming paste. Specialist shops supply liming wax, but this cannot be sealed. Instead you could use a white emulsion thickened with a little plaster of Paris, as in the example here. Work the paste into the wood with a brush and then rub it off with a rag, leaving the wood to dry pale and ghostlike. Apply a sand sealer*, and when this is dry, gently sand the surface with a fine paper*. Protect the effect with an extra pale varnish*. A splatter of black is sometimes added to suggest age.

✱ Further information

Pickling *p.84*
Equipment *p.22*
Preparation *p.19*
Sanding *p.21*
Varnishing *p.29*

Equipment

White emulsion or latex
Plaster of Paris
Paint kettle
Paste application brush
Wire brush
Sand sealer
Sealer application brush
Fine sandpaper
Rags
Varnish (extra pale)
Varnish brush
Black emulsion and spatter brush (optional)

1 Open the pores of the wood by brushing along the grain with a wire brush.

2 Apply a coat of liming paste mixed from white emulsion and plaster of Paris, working it well into the raw wood.

3 Use a clean dry rag to remove the excess paste.

6 Varnishing brings the finish alive, revealing how the grain has picked up the white flecks of liming paste.

4 Apply the sand sealer with a suitable brush and allow to dry.

5 Sand the piece with a very fine paper to create an ultra-smooth finish for varnishing.

7 This technique is ideal for chairs, tables and picture frames.

Malachite

Equipment

Oil glaze coloured with viridian

Oil glaze coloured with monestial green

Oil glaze coloured with blue-black

White spirit

Artist's round brush

Stencil brush

Malachite is a rich green mineral formed of copper carbonate, named because its colour resembles that of mallow leaves, and noted for its circular "bull's-eye" veining. Found in Eastern Europe, malachite has been used to great effect in Russian architecture, but is more often seen elsewhere as jewellery or as a decorative addition to furniture. Like all natural substances, malachite occurs in differing shades ranging from aqua green to emerald, and the bands of colour which overlap to make its characteristic bull's-eyes, vary from one stone to another. This effect has often been simulated in the past, using brushes and combs. The technique shown only employs brushes, in order to achieve a more muted result.

The ground colour should be a pale blue-green. When this has dried hard, check the surface for faults and fine-sand it* before top coating. Apply a viridian oil glaze* and swirl it around with an artist's round brush*. Experiment with this swirling technique, overlapping the whirls until the entire surface is covered and the snaking patterns begin to build up into an overall design.

Next, introduce a second oil-based glaze tinted with darker monestial green. Work this into the still-wet veridian glaze to produce depths and shallows which begin to mix and blur. Form complete bull's-eyes by twisting the brush gently in a circle. Slight judder is quite acceptable – in fact these circles should not be perfect. Now attack the glazes with white spirit, drawn carefully with a brush along one or two of the tracks already made in the glaze. The resulting patterns, which look like the contours on a map of some mythical land, should then be highlighted and strengthened with blue-black glaze and a spattering* of white spirit. This will suggest changing depths and bring into play a more natural figuring. The

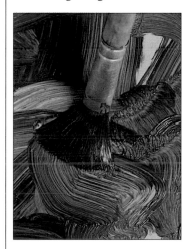

1 Apply the viridian glaze in a haphazard way, manipulating the brush to move the colour about over the surface.

2 Using the artist's round brush, start to make the swirling marks. Hold the brush at the very tip, and roll it between finger and thumb to change direction. In this way, tight manoeuvres can be made quite easily. This is a good time to play with the glaze and experiment with different shapes. There is no pressure of time. The glaze will take a while to begin tacking off. If it does, you can remove and re-apply it.

surface will now be very wet, and must be allowed to dry thoroughly before varnishing.

✳ Further information

Sanding *p.21*

Mixing glazes *p.13*

Mediums *p.10*

Brushes *p.24*

Spattering *p.96*

3 The monestial green glaze now comes into play, applied in a similar way to the viridian. At this point a vague scheme should be evolving. The monestial glaze should cover about 80 percent of the area, leaving the viridian to glow in shallows and highlight the figuring.

6 The blue-black will help to accentuate an impression of changing depths and white spirit spattered on with a stencil brush will give a less contrived feel to the effect.

7 Using a stencil brush loaded with white spirit, retrace some of the lines previously made. The glaze will dissolve and show the ground colour through a veil of green. Introduce some blue-black glaze to the pattern, especially in the bull's-eyes.

4 Create bull's-eyes of different sizes by twisting the brush between finger and thumb. Do not rush – a quick movement tends to introduce straight lines, which are disastrous to this finish.

5 The circular tracks, like mysterious contours on some undersea map, should meander around and under the bull's-eyes and each other.

8 The completed effect shows the degree of depth which can be achieved with this finish.

Marbling

Siena marble

◆

Black and gold marble

◆

Egyptian green marble

Marbling is the finishing of a surface in close imitation of real marble, and will therefore be more successful if you study the figuring and veining of at least a few standard marbles.

Marbling dates back to ancient Egypt, and is said to owe its evolution to the high cost of the genuine material and the difficulty of transporting it over large distances. However, the art spread, even in countries such as France and Italy where marble was easily available. The reason probably lies in the nature of marble itself. A strong compacted stone, it is a safe building material when used in a block or column. But it cannot be used for beams and ceilings. These would therefore be decorated with the faux finish to complete a marble room scheme.

Similar techniques were also employed in a purely decorative way to create pleasing marble-like effects without regard for authenticity. This fantasy marbling, known today as marblizing, was used in harpsichord cases and other situations where it would obviously be impossible to use the true material. The techniques shown here have been passed down over many years specifically to produce imitations of real marble. But skills you acquire while practising these effects can equally well be used with any colour combination you like to produce a marblizing effect.

Siena marble

This marble is warm and delicately figured, and lends itself to use on walls and skirtings, or furniture. Prepare the surface well*, and apply a white oil-based ground coat*, which must be hard dry before further coating. Add an even coat of matt white oil-based undercoat tinted with raw sienna artists' oil colour.

Now mix three tinted oil glazes with the following artists' oil colours: raw sienna, burnt sienna and vermilion. Lay the three glazes onto the wet ground in fairly uneven patches. Blot the three colours with a crushed rag. Then use the hog-hair softening brush* to blend the colours into the wet ground. This is an important technique to practise, as it is employed in most marble effects, as well as in graining* and tortoise-shelling*.

Dampen the sword brush* with white spirit and load it with blue-black oil colour to draw in the veins. When the main veins are in place soften them with a badger-hair brush*, Distress* the ground here and there, using a marine sponge* and white spirit. Then soften

again, this time with a hog-hair brush*. Add the cloudy white deposits by softly applying thin white undercoat with a sword liner and softening with a hog-hair brush. Put in the fractured secondary veining using the sword liner and blue-black, softening from time to time. Add white veins and highlights without softening.

Allow the completed marble to dry. Varnish*, and then wet-and-dry* until flat. Touch in any lost detail or highlights and varnish again using an extra pale varnish*.

Equipment

White undercoat
White undercoat tinted with raw sienna
Oil glaze mix tinted with raw sienna
Oil glaze mix tinted with burnt sienna
Oil glaze mix tinted with vermilion
Blue-black artists' oil colour
Four application brushes
Hog-hair softening brush
Badger-hair softening brush
Sword brush (also called a liner or striper)
Marine sponge
Lint-free cotton rags
White spirit

✱ Further information

Preparation *p.17*
Mediums *p.10*
Mixing colours *p.13*
Brushes *p.24*
Graining *p.63*
Tortoiseshell *p.111*
Distressing *p.43*
Marine sponges *p.26*
Sanding *p.21*
Finishing marble *p.80*
Varnishing *p.29*

The ground
1 Evenly apply the white undercoat tinted with raw sienna.

3 Add some similarly sized patches of vermilion tinted glaze.

5 Use the lint-free rag to blot the wet surface.

2 The brush must be kept clean throughout. Rub it onto a clean, dry rag before you soften the ground to the north, and repeat the cleaning every time you change direction.

2 While the ground is wet, lay on patches of burnt sienna tinted glaze.

4 The raw sienna tinted glaze completes the tri-colour combination.

Softening
1 Soften the ground colours with the hog-hair softener. This technique is worked in four directions – north, south, east and west. Here the brush is being gently drawn to the south. The bristles should barely touch the surface, and the brush should be angled slightly towards the direction in which it is travelling.

3 Soften in an easterly and then a westerly direction, remembering to clean the brush constantly.

4 If the brush is used too strongly brushmarks will appear. This can be put right by cleaning the brush and brushing lightly at right angles to the mark. Here the final softening strokes are being applied. Compare the appearance of the ground now to the way it looked at the start of softening.

2 Soften the veins in the same way as the ground colours, but this time using a badger-hair softener. The finest of all brushes, this will soften so delicately that the subtleness achieved is breathtaking.

4 Soften the sponged areas following the same technique as before, brushing the slanted hog-haired softener gently to the north, south, east and west.

6 Soften with the hog-hair brush, first along the vein, then gently away from it, and finally back towards the vein. In this way, the chalky deposits appear to be held back by the veins.

Veining

1 Using the sword brush dampened with white spirit, pick up some blue-black and draw the major veins quite quickly. Always pull the brush towards you, and change direction by twisting it between finger and thumb. Here a forking vein is drawn, broken by the kind of crack which is typical of marble.

3 Using a natural marine sponge slightly dampened in white spirit, gently dab over the ground. This technique causes the ground to burn through in places and create a freckled effect which contrasts well with the smoky softness of the other areas.

5 Use the sword brush to apply patches of white undercoat. These should be bounded by a vein as shown.

7 Draw in the finely cracked and splintered secondary veins, using the sword brush and blue-black.

9 Use white undercoat for additional veining detail and to highlight veins and cracks.

10 The completed Siena marble should be varnished when dry to protect and enhance the delicacy of the effect.*

8 These cracks form on every bend of a vein, and fracture forwards as well as backwards, creating a fine web-like network. The crack shown in the first veining pictures appears here in greater detail, and has led to further crazing, which stops only when it joins the next main vein. This type of structure is common in marble, where veining results from enormous changes in temperature and pressure that crystallize colour and fragment the limestone from which it is formed.

Black and gold marble

An exotic marble with fiery veins and speckles of gold and white, this has often been used for skirtings, especially in contrast to walls of a paler marble. It would make a good choice for lamps and table-tops.

The ground must be black, dense and smooth, and the effect is achieved with brush, feather and sponge. Begin figuring with patches of yellow ochre oil glaze* and Venetian red* from which fibrous veins will extend. Apply them in a two-colour brushing technique using a sword brush, or striper*. Load this with the yellow ochre glaze, but add a little Venetian red straight from the tube to the top part of the bristles, or heel of the brush, nearest the stock. In this way, you can put in touches of red when required simply by lowering the heel of the brush onto the surface. This may take a little practice, but adds greatly to the effect.

Apply fine white veins with a feather – any kind will do providing it's clean*. Use the wide edge, which will hold more paint and produce a finer line. Then soften the marble to north, south, east and west with the badger-hair brush*, as for Siena marble*. Dampen the marine sponge* in a little white spirit, and bounce it gingerly over the veining to produce a freckled, slightly pitted effect. Work over this, using an artist's writing brush and the sword brush to fiddle in more veins and achieve a faintly honeycomb effect. Highlight this with white and an occasional hint of red before softening again. Put in the fine highlights with an artist's brush and leave the piece to dry. Finish the marbling by applying an extra pale varnish*.

Equipment

*Oil glaze tinted with
yellow ochre
Venetian red artists' oil colour
White undercoat
Sword brush
Feather
Badger-hair softening brush
Artist's writing brush
Marine sponge
White spirit
Fine wet-and-dry paper
Extra pale varnish and
application brush
Clean rags*

✳ Further information

Mixing glazes *p.13*
Mediums *p.10*
Brushes *p.24*
Feathers *p.26*
Softening technique *p.76*
Marine sponge *p.26*
Varnishing *p.29*
Finishing marble *p.81*

1 Apply the yellow ochre glaze with the sword brush, pulling and fidgeting the brush while twisting it between finger and thumb.

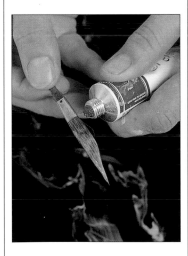

2 Dab Venetian red artists' oil colour onto the heel of the brush so that from time to time during the figuring you can add a trace of red to enhance the fiery look characteristic of this marble.

3 Dance the brush along and allow the heel to make gentle contact with the ground to deposit some red.

4 Use the feather (in this case, a goose feather) to draw in fine white veins running with and against the trend.

5 Add the white to the major veins, using the broader side of the feather, which will hold more paint and produce a thinner line.

6 Soften the entire area with the badger brush, remembering to work in each of the four directions in turn and to keep the brush clean and dry by rubbing with a rag.

8 Strengthen the main figure using the yellow ochre on an artist's writing brush.

10 Use the sword brush to put white veins and highlights into the main figure. Add a few touches of red before softening again with the badger brush.

7 Dampen the marine sponge slightly with white spirit, and pounce it gently over the central figure. Holes will appear where the white spirit dissolves the glaze.

9 A honeycomb structure begins to evolve as the figuring continues.

11 When figuring is complete, add the final touches of white. Do not soften any further.

12 The finished effect has a powerful starkness warmed by the impression of inner fire.

FINISHING MARBLE

1 All marble effects must be varnished* to seal and enhance the finish. Allow the surface to dry completely – normally for 24 to 48 hours – before sealing with a first coat of oil varnish. Then use fine wet-and-dry paper and a block*, together with water, to smooth the surface*.

2 Apply a protective coating of extra pale varnish with a varnish brush*. Further coats can be added according to the degree of finish required.

3 The completed effect shows how the varnish brings the finish into focus and adds an important layer of depth.

Egyptian green marble

This rich dark green marble is often used on pilasters and plinths, but its intricate detail and luxurious quality make it appropriate for smaller items such as table-tops and inlays.

The effect begins with a black ground, which should be smooth and dense. Use a toothbrush or short-bristled brush to spatter* vermilion oil glaze* lightly over this surface. When this has tacked off roll on terre verte glaze with an artist's writing brush*. Twist the brush between the finger and thumb to roll the glaze off it. When about three-quarters of the area is covered with terre verte glaze, soften the effect with a crushed newspaper. Now fiddle in the white veins. These should be softened every so often using the badger-hair brush*. Gradually the dark green ground begins to break up beneath the fine web of veins. Touches of vermilion highlight some of the small plates surrounded by veining. Soften these, and allow the surface to dry before smoothing and varnishing with extra pale varnish*.

Equipment

Oil glaze mix tinted with vermilion
Oil glaze mix tinted with terre verte
White undercoat
Toothbrush or stencil brush
Artist's writing brush
Artist's 00 brush
Badger-hair softening brush
Sword brush
Newspaper
Cotton rags

✳ Further information

Spattering *p.96*
Mixing glazes *p.13*
Mediums *p.10*
Brushes *p.24*
Varnishing *p.29*
Sponging *p.98*
Ragging *p.88*
Softening technique *p.76*
Siena marble *p.75*

Initial effects
1 Using a toothbrush or stencil brush, spatter the vermilion glaze onto the black ground and allow to tack off.

2 Twist the artist's writing brush between finger and thumb to roll the terre verte glaze onto the ground.

3 Roll the brush this way and that while drawing it over the surface until about three-quarters of the area is covered.

Veining

1 While the ground is still wet, apply the white undercoat thinned with white spirit or turpentine substitute, using the sword brush.* Again, roll the brush between finger and thumb, and use its flat, tapered shape to produce wide and narrow vein lines. Make all your painting strokes towards the body, bringing the width and the heel of the brush into play when a broad vein is required and the tip and edge of the brush for a thin vein.

4 Soften the effect by crushing the newspaper into a pad and working over the surface as if you were sponging* or ragging.*

2 When the initial veins are in, soften them with the badger brush. The softening gives a smoky effect, and creates the illusion that the vein is a little way under the surface.

3 Add more veins, like this one, sketched over the top of an earlier vein. The meandering veins of this marble differ quite strongly from the patterns found in the Siena marble*.

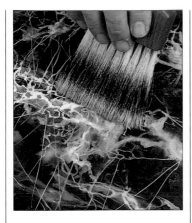

4 More softening follows, and you can see the gradual build-up of fine, straight crack veins which run at right angles to the original trend.

Softening
1 Some of the small plates created as the white veins break up the surface are picked up with vermilion from an artist's 00 brush.

3 Only a clean brush will produce a good quality finish. Clean the bristles regularly with a dry rag.

2 Soften the vermilion plates using the badger-hair brush. As always, softening is crucial to successful marbling. The bristles should hardly touch the surface.

4 The completed surface showing the swirling, frothy network of veins intersected by fine lines. Allow this to dry before varnishing. Varnish enriches the shading and preserves the texture of the finished effect.

Pickling

Equipment
Sand sealer
3 brushes
White emulsion/latex
Rag
Fine glasspaper
Varnish (extra pale)

This effect dates back to a finish called pickle pine, which evolved in the late 19th century. At the time, paint was commonly used to conceal the cheap construction of much of the pine, or deal, furniture to be found in the servants' quarters and among the less well off. But the emergence of the Arts and Crafts movement fuelled a fashion for natural wood, and stripping painted pine became increasingly popular. The stripping was a highly dangerous treatment undertaken with nitric acid. This left the wood looking aged and ashen, with white or grey remnants of paint and gesso clinging to the crevices. In some cases, the wood lost its colour and resembled driftwood. In others, the colour was darkened.

This "soft on the eye" effect (which came about by accident) was so admired that soon a technique was developed to apply it to new furniture. This involved bleaching and staining the wood, followed by filling the grain with a white or grey paint or paste. By the 1930s the effect was being used extensively, and cheap short-cuts were replacing the genuine technique for treating new wood. In a similar way to the evolution of graining*, the cheap, quick and badly applied effects found their way into restaurants and public houses, and out of favour.

Today the effect can be undertaken with little risk, as no acid is employed. And although purists may continue to view it with some disdain, its pale chalky demeanour and the ease with which it enables a piece to fit into a colour scheme have guaranteed pickling, like liming*, a resurgence in popularity.

The piece to be finished should be in a raw state, and free of grease and grime. If the wood is very pale you can stain it at this stage to provide some contrast with the top coat. Next you should seal with a sand sealer. This is a clear shellac* with a methylated-spirit base, so it will soon be dry. Brush on a white emulsion* and remove it with a rag, leaving the surface relatively clean, except for crevices and corners, which naturally trap the paint. Work on one area at a time, or the emulsion will dry before it is wiped off. When wiping is complete, allow the piece to dry, sand it thoroughly, and protect it with one or two coats of extra pale varnish*.

✱ Further information
Graining *p. 63*
Liming *p. 71*
Mediums *p.10*
Sanding/abrasive paper
chart *p.21*
Varnishing *p.29*

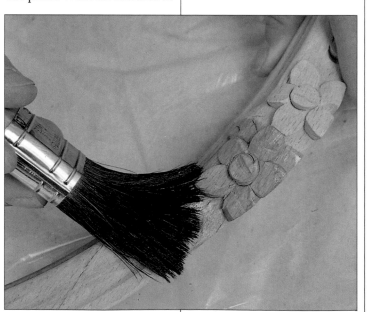

1 Clean the surface and apply sand sealer with a brush. The sealer will quickly be absorbed by the wood.

2 When the wood is dry, apply a white emulsion or latex* by brush, ensuring that every nook and cranny is covered).

4 When the piece is dry, sand it with a fine-grade paper*, remembering to go with the grain.

3 Wipe the emulsion off the majority of the surface – only the detailing will readily retain the paint. The emulsion will dry quite quickly, so work on small areas at a time, applying and wiping, rather than trying to cover the whole piece and then wiping it.

5 Apply one or two coats of extra pale varnish to protect and enhance the effect.

6 This chalky, clean looking effect readily lends itself to a variety of wide ranging decorating schemes and is justly popular with designers and decorators.

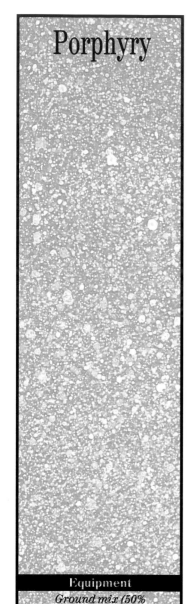

Porphyry

Porphyry is a very hard variegated igneous rock with a granite-like texture, often containing fool's gold. Although it occurs in different colours, such as green and reddish-brown, it is best known in its predominantly purple form, and its name means "purple stone". The Romans particularly enjoyed this exquisite colour, and dubbed the rock the "imperial purple porphyry" because its colour betokened imperial rank. The effect is, therefore, a faux finish, for which it is advisable to look at an original beforehand, as in the case of marbling* or graining*. It is best used on plinths, columns and anywhere suitable for genuine porphyry.

The technique involves two basic finishes: the ground coat, which is sponged off*; and the glaze or top coat, which is spattered*. Undertake the initial spattering by loading a long-haired brush with colour that has been thinned to the consistency of milk. Tap the brush with the spatter stick, or vice versa. The stick has no other purpose, so almost any scrap of wood will do in its place. The impact between stick and brush will cause the bristles to flick strongly and discharge the colour droplets.

Porphyry uses oil-based glazes and mediums*. The ground coat colour is mixed using ultramarine, cadmium red and a little lamp black, together with transparent oil glaze, thinned with white spirit. It is advisable to use artists' oils, which are of higher quality, and to mix a strong colour, which will be more permanent. The ratio of colour to glaze will dictate the strength of the colour.

✱ Further information

Marbling *p.75*
Graining *p.63*
Sponging off *p.103*
Spattering *p.96*
Mediums *p.10*

Equipment

Ground mix (50% ultramarine, 50% cadmium red, with glaze and white spirit, touch lamp black)
Brush
Synthetic sponge
Spattering brush
Spattering stick
White glaze
Gold glaze

1 Apply the colour-mixed glaze to the surface with a brush.

2 Using a clean, dry, synthetic sponge, even out the glaze and remove the brush marks. Pounce the sponge over the area*.

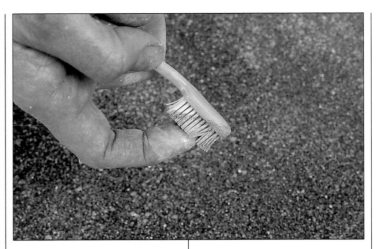

5 The addition of a gold spatter to imitate the fool's gold often found in porphyry complements the effect.

6 The finished effect imitates the rich colour of the real stone to perfection.

3 Load the spattering brush of your choice with white, oil-based undercoat, thinned with white spirit to the consistency of milk. Tap the brush against the spatter stick, releasing speckles of paint onto the ground.

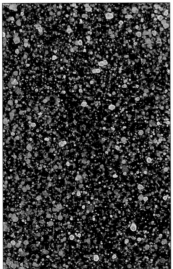

4 The combination of the fine drawn-up pinnacles of stipple and the white spots of spatter is an attractive finish in its own right.

Ragging

Rag rolling

◆

Bagging

◆

Ragging on and frosting

◆

Gold and silver fossil

Ragging covers a selection of finishes which rely on the contours of fabric. The fabrics used range from linen to plastic, and their effects are dramatic and diverse. Colours for this effect are normally soft, and the base colour is nearly always the paler one. The obvious exception is frosting*, which is achieved with a white or off-white top coat. The majority of the effects are subtracted* and therefore require a certain amount of planning when large areas are to be finished.

The procedures needed for ragging, and their results, vary in two respects. First there is an enormous choice of materials, from paper to chamois leather, each of which will give a different texture. Second is the way in which the chosen material is manipulated – whether rolled across the surface or pounced in a similar way to stippling. The application of the top coat can be by brush or roller. If you use a brush be careful to lay off* the glaze and therefore lessen the brush marks. Some finished effects can be quite open and would be spoiled by such visible marks. The effect is one of the most dramatic and can be used for a wide variety of purposes. The crushed velvet texture can take on a marble-like appearance, especially when a grey or stone colour is used as the base and paler mid-tone as a top coat. Many a coffee table has been improved with this technique.

Rag rolling

This effect is produced by rolling a lint-free rag over the wet surface of the glaze. Any material can be used, providing it is lint-free and clean, and unlikely to bleed colour. Towelling will create a soft texture, while a non-absorbent plastic bag will leave a sharp, well-defined look. Most important when choosing your material is its quantity. If you are finishing a large room, you will need a plentiful stock of material, so that sodden rags can be replaced.

The preparation should be of good quality, but rag-rolling is kind to its surface. This makes it especially appropriate for a wall that is sound but has undulated as old walls often do. Unlike dragging*, which would highlight the lumps and bumps, rag-rolling will make these less apparent.

Many techniques have been offered over the years to achieve this effect, but the original procedure has yet to be bettered. The technique is to crush the fabric several times by screwing it up and then unravelling it. This will give it some initial character. The material is then gathered into a loose bunch and rolled in a diagonal course over the surface with the lightest of pressure. Avoid using the rag tightly rolled as this produces a repeated pattern and heightens the danger of skidding. Try to fill the area without rolling vertically or horizontally, as the eye will pick this up and the finish will be marred. Once you have covered an area, stand back and blur your eyes to check for dark patches. These can be blotted to keep the undulating effect even.

When you have completed the work or are taking a break, be sure to spread or hang out the used rags that have glaze mix on them, so that they dry thoroughly.

Equipment

Paint or glaze
Brush or roller
Rags

✳ Further information

Frosting *p.90*
Applied and subtracted finishes *p.15*
Applying mediums *p.16*
Dragging *p.54*
Ragging on *p.90*

WARNING

Never be tempted to throw rags away wet or leave them bunched up, because they are highly inflammable and can ignite spontaneously.

1 Apply the glaze – in strips of about 60 cm (24 in) wide for a large area.

2 Lay off* the glaze lightly, spreading it out and eliminating brush marks.

4 Blot darker areas and check the evenness of the finish by standing away from it and blurring your eyes. Lighter areas or bald patches may be remedied by ragging on* a little glaze with a wet rag.

3 Roll the loosely bunched rag across the surface in a diagonal direction, applying only delicate pressure. Fill in, using angled runs, avoiding the vertical and the horizontal.

5 The completed rag-roll effect should tumble and twist across the surface. Viewed from a distance, the movement should be soft and not patchy.

Bagging

Bagging, or bag stippling is one of the simplest subtracted* effects. The choice of medium is limited to a transparent oil glaze, because a solvent is sometimes required to break up the glazed surface. A brown paper bag dipped into white spirit or turpentine substitute and scrunched up gives a crackled effect. Plastic bags are also used, and the thicker and more robust the bag the crisper the effect. A relatively soft supermarket bag was used in this example, which produced a subdued texture. Bagging is a soft, luxurious effect which, in some colours, can look like marble. It is best suited to smaller areas, woodwork, or on the walls of an opulent dining room.

Equipment
Glaze
Brush or roller
Paper or plastic bag

✳ Further information
Applied and subtracted finishes *p.15*
Applying mediums *p.16*

1 Apply the glaze with a brush or roller.

2 Spread out the medium, and lay off* to reduce brush marks.

3 Pounce the bag over the surface. it is unlikely that more than one bag will be needed, because very little glaze is picked up by the plastic – it is merely redistributed.

4 The finished effect is luxurious, relying almost entirely on texture rather than the contrast between the ground and top coat.

Ragging on and frosting

Unlike the other rag effects, these are applied finishes*. The glaze is applied to the dry ground or base coat with a rag. The choice of rag is wide, but it must be reasonably porous in order to carry the glaze.

Ragging on
Ragging on probably evolved from rag rolling*, where it is often used to correct an error. Suitable colours are closely linked to those for sponging on*, as is the technique. The effect can be achieved with any glaze, but water-based glazes are most often chosen because of their quick drying. The only tools you need are those for preparation, together with a rag, some glaze, and a card for testing. Dip the rag into the glaze and test its print on the card. Once you have an acceptable print, you are ready to approach your surface. The effect needs to be built up gradually, and because this is an applied effect, you can stop at any time and resume at a later date. The technique is the same as for sponging on*, with the rag taking the place of the sponge. As an applied

finish, ragging on has obvious advantages. In addition, it provides a sharp, more aggressive contrast between the ground and the top coats. The finish is often used on walls, but with very soft colours to make the overall effect easier on the eye.

Frosting
Frosting is a finish that works to great effect over many different grounds. It is achieved by either sponging on or ragging on, and is frequently used to refinish a decorative scheme quickly and inexpensively. It is often applied over paint effects that need lifting because they have become too heavy. A white or off-white top coat, put on by rag or sponge, is gradually worked up, as described in sponging on*, until it almost conceals the original surface. Although technically a colour reversal of two other effects, frosting is widely regarded by decorators as a finish in its own right.

1 The white glaze is here applied with crumpled paper.

2 You should cover the whole area and gradually build it up, taking time to step back regularly and check the patches.

3 The completed effect is crisp, reminiscent of a frosty morning.

Equipment
Glaze or paint
Rag or paper
Card

* Further information
Applied and subtracted finishes *p.15*
Rag rolling *p.88*
Sponging on *p.98*

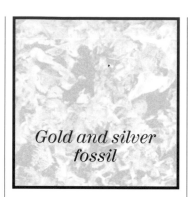

Gold and silver fossil

These effects, named for their appearance, are very much part of the rag finishes. The technique is the same as that for ragging* and rag rolling*, but the glazes are different. The effect is luxurious, and should, therefore, be used sparingly. It is normally confined to furniture and accessories. Emulsion glaze* is used for both finishes, mixed with bronze powder for the gold effect or aluminium powder for the silver, and thinned slightly. The base coat should be a dead flat black and good preparation is important. The surface must be very smooth.

Gold
Lay the gold glaze onto the ground coat with a brush. Roll a piece of mutton cloth across the surface but press firmly. The fine powder will adhere to the ground, and the medium will be absorbed by the rag. Take care as you roll to push or pull the gold mixture into a pleasing effect. The holes in the mutton cloth will contribute to this, and the bits of lint left on the surface can be removed when dry.

A spattered effect can be added to the damp glaze with the aid of methylated spirit (see silver glaze).

Silver
Aluminium powder is mixed into the emulsion glaze in the same way as the bronze powder, but needs a slightly thinner mix, produced by adding more water. The application – again only by brush – should be quickly followed by the ragging technique. Use a cotton cloth, twisting it slightly while it is pounced to produce a good print. At this point, you can create a further effect by spattering methylated spirit over the area. This releases the glaze in spots and pools, an effect that can also be achieved with the bronze glaze.

Equipment
Emulsion glazes
Paint kettle
Water
Bronze powder (Rich pale gold) or
Aluminium powder
Brush
Mutton cloth
Toothbrush
Rag
Methylated spirit
Stick

✱ Further information
Ragging *p.88*
Rag rolling *p.88*
Mediums *p.10*
Equipment *p.22*
Varnishing *p.29*

Gold
1 Pour the emulsion glaze into a paint kettle and add a little bronze powder.

3 Do not allow the mixture to become thicker than single cream.

2 Mix the powder and glaze with a little water and continue adding bronze powder a small amount at a time.

4 Apply the glaze with a brush. Do not spread too thinly.

Silver

1 Use a brush to apply the glaze, which should be slightly thinner than its gold counterpart.

3 Use an old toothbrush to spatter the still-wet surface with methylated spirit.

5 Rag roll the area with mutton cloth, exerting a firm pressure to move the glaze.

6 When the surface is dry, the lint from the mutton cloth can be rubbed off, leaving an undulating, luxurious finish, which should be protected with a glass or satin varnish*.

2 Rag the glaze in a pouncing movement, using a lightly screwed-up piece of cotton. Apply some pressure to the rag and slightly skid or twist it if it becomes difficult to acquire a good print.

4 The finished effect is almost molten in texture, ideal for an art deco style interior.

Sandstone and Lichen

While faux stone blocks* have moved from being an exterior finish to grace many a fine entrance hall or stairwell, the related sandstone and lichen effect finds its natural environment outside in the oramentation of garden or summerhouse. Lichen can be encouraged to grow on new stoneware by painting it with live yoghurt, but this takes time. An instant effect using paint can be remarkably effective. The example here is a Bacchus corbel (a decorative masonry support) made of polyurethane foam. It is first painted with a dull ochre oil-based ground*. When this is dry, a thin white emulsion glaze is scumbled (scrubbing dry paint with a dry brush over another dry layer) over the piece, which is then stippled* with a raw sienna wash while still wet*. The surface is gently ragged* to leave the yellow ground in some areas, and the white or sienna in others. The white glaze is then reapplied using a marine sponge*. This sponging* must be done delicately, allowing the sponge* merely to settle on the surface rather than pushing it into the hollows. The lichen is applied by spattering* yellow ochre and opaque oxide of chromium* onto the wet surface. The effect should be sealed with a matt water-based sealer*, as any sheen would be inconsistent with sandstone.

Equipment

White emulsion glaze and coarse application brush
Raw sienna wash and application brush
Yellow ochre and opaque oxide of chromium (acrylic colours)
Matt water-based sealer and brush
Marine sponge
Spatter brush
Cotton rag

✱ Further information

Faux stone blocks *p.59*
Mediums *p.10*
Mixing glazes *p.13*
Stippling *p.104*
Colour washes *p.47*
Ragging *p.88*
Marine sponges *p.26*
Sponging *p.98*
Spattering *p.96*
Mediums chart *p.10*
Varnishing *p.29*

1 When the dull yellow ground is dry, apply the thin white emulsion glaze using a coarse emulsion brush to produce a patchy undulating coat.

2 Stipple the raw sienna wash into all the crevices, and haphazardly over the surface, missing some areas altogether.

5 Simulate the lichen by spattering yellow ochre and opaque oxide of chromium onto the wet surface.

3 Rag the surface with a crumpled piece of cotton. This softens the two colours and allows the ground to show through in some areas.

4 Reapply the white very gently, using the marine sponge. Treat the entire piece, allowing the undulations to dictate the areas coated.

6 Protect the completed piece with a matt water-based sealer to preserve the natural appearance of the effect.

Spattering

Equipment

Ground coat
Brush or roller
Paints or glazes (thinned)
Spatter brush
Card
Paint kettle
Stick

This effect has a subtlety that enables it to be used in practically all aspects of paint finishing – from marbling* to antiquing*, from sharpening a dull effect to calming a vivid colour. The tools and brushes needed to execute the effect are cheap and easy to acquire, and all mediums mentioned in this book, including varnish and ink, can be used with great success.

Spattering gets its name from the way in which the medium is conveyed onto the chosen surface. The resulting spots of colour call to mind the work of artists like Seurat. Before deciding on a colour combination for your spatter, take time to look at some pointillist paintings to see how colours in dot form work when placed next to one another.

Glaze and brushes
Success of application relies on the thickness of the paint or glaze. Thin down your chosen pre-tinted medium with a relevant thinner to the consistency of milk. The choice of brush is enormous – from a toothbrush to a dusting brush. The most commonly used brushes are stencil brushes* and worn fitches*.

Spatter can be applied to a dry or a wet ground, using a short-bristled brush, as described here, or a long-haired brush and a spatter stick (see Porphyry*). For the short-bristled method, you can use a toothbrush, stencil brush, or any short-bristled brush. Load the brush with thinned colour and draw your finger or a knife-blade over the bristles so that they flick fine spots of colour onto the surface. If the glaze is too thick, the brush will not release it. If it is too thin, or the brush overloaded, the spots will run down the surface and will need to be removed. It

Multicoloured spatter on a dry ground
1 Mix the colour with the appropriate thinner to the consistency of milk.

2 Lightly load the brush, and hold it so that the colour runs to the ends of the bristles and not toward the stock. Slowly pull your finger over the ends of the bristles, so that small spots of colour are propelled onto the surface.

3 Once the spatter is dry, you can apply a second colour, in this case gold.

is a wise precaution to try out the effect on a test card first, as in sponging on*. Spatter the surface in an overall manner. Do not hold the brush too near the surface, as this will lead to patches and heighten the danger of runs.

The short-bristled method will give a finely speckled effect, the size of spots depending to some extent on your distance from the surface and your particular way of handling the brush. If you work on a dry ground, there will be no pressure to finish the spatter quickly, and when one layer is dry, you can add another.

A wet ground offers you a more dynamic look with less likelihood of runs.

The disadvantage of this effect – whether you are finishing a room or a small piece – is that the spatter tends to go everywhere. So dust-sheeting is essential. If you wear glasses, cover the lenses with cling film.

Spatter on a wet ground
This finish changes the fine salt-and-pepper texture of dry ground spatter into a more effervescent effect. Whereas the spots of colour on a dry ground remain in their concentrated state on the surface, a wet ground allows the colour particles to infiltrate. Because a wet ground is being used, the finish now becomes a subtracted effect, and all the rules for subtracted finishes* apply. Oil-based glaze is recommended due to its slower drying.

✳ Further information
Marbling *p. 75*
Antiquing *p. 34*
Brushes/Equipment *p. 22*
Porphyry *p. 86*
Sponging on *p. 98*
Applied and subtracted finishes *p. 15*

---

4 The completed effect has a feeling of depth, and the gold dots glint like tiny sequins.

Spatter on a wet ground
1 Apply the ground coat by brush or roller.

3 The finished effect, showing how the spatter has soaked into the live ground coat. Compare this with the totally different effect created on a dry ground.

2 Spatter the thinned glaze, following the same method as for the dry ground. Because the ground is wet, the spatter is less likely to run.

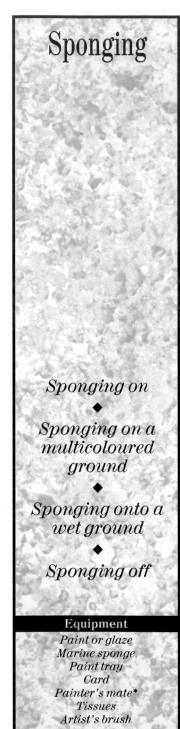

Sponging

Sponging on

◆

Sponging on a multicoloured ground

◆

Sponging onto a wet ground

◆

Sponging off

Equipment

*Paint or glaze
Marine sponge
Paint tray
Card
Painter's mate*
Tissues
Artist's brush*

Sponging on

Sponging on is probably the simplest of all the paint effects, in that paint or glaze is applied to the surface rather than removed from it. Except in blended finishes*, drying time has no bearing on the final effect. This means you do not have to rush. Sponging techniques are straightforward and it is relatively easy to achieve an extremely effective finish. It is important to select a good marine sponge. This will have a large proportion of frills, rather than consisting mainly of holes. Marine sponges are not cheap, so ask to inspect a number of them before making your choice. Bear in mind the area you wish to finish: the bigger the sponge, the less time it will take to cover a large surface. Make sure that you have all your equipment to hand before you start.

Sponging can be done with oil- or water-based mediums. An oil-based glaze will produce an opulent, marble-like effect; a water-based glaze will be softer and chalkier. A water-based medium was chosen for the example shown below. Because it dries more quickly, it is less likely to be smudged by accident.

First, dampen your sponge with water. This will allow it to expand to its natural shape and also reduce its absorbency. Only the sponge's contours are required for this effect, not its ability to absorb the medium. In fact the more it absorbs, the sooner it will need to be cleaned. Decant the medium (emulsion) into the paint tray. Tip the tray so that a wave of paint or glaze runs up onto the ramp of the tray and back, leaving a film of paint or glaze. Load the sponge and test it by printing onto the card. When a pleasing print has been achieved, apply in a haphazard fashion over the area. Cover the area roughly at first, then fill in.

To avoid smudges, refrain from working on adjacent walls. Allow one wall to dry before going on to its

1 Take the dampened sponge and load the frilly side with colour by dabbing it onto the ramp.

2 Test the print of the sponge on the card. If only fine specks are apparent, more paint or glaze is needed. If a muddy wet print is left, too much paint or glaze has been picked up, and you should print off the excess before starting.

neighbour, and leave a random edge on either side of every internal corner.

Rectifying errors
When an error occurs, such as a blob where too much paint or glaze has been applied, or a twist where the sponge has been turned while still in contact with the surface, blot the excess with a tissue and allow to dry. Carefully touch in the ground or base colour over any top colour that has extended too far, or that appears pale and smudged. When the ground colour is dry, you can apply the top colour again.

✱ Further information
Equipment *p.22*

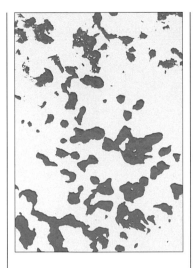

4 Change the angle of the sponge frequently to avoid a potato-print effect. Always test your sponge on the card after recharging with medium.

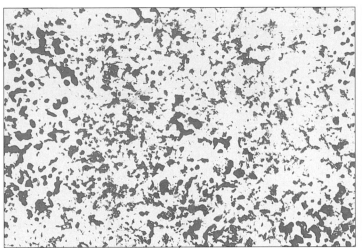

6 The completed effect should be as uniform as you can make it, naturally gaining a movement which should have no direction.

3 Once a crisp, open print has been achieved, apply this in a haphazard fashion over the area. Do not work from one side to the other, or the overall effect will be patchy.

5 Step away from the surface occasionally and remove your glasses, or blur your vision. This will enable you to spot lighter areas where extra prints are needed.

7 The two-colour sponge-on effect is achieved by repeating the process, in this case with a softer colour, which breaks up the strong colour into a more fractured effect.

Corners

1 When sponging walls, leave a random edge on either side of corners, using a painter's mate to shield the neighbouring surface as you work. Leave the area to dry.

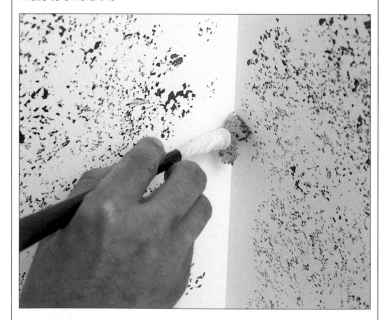

2 Use a piece of sponge taped to the end of a stick or long-handled artist's brush to sponge in the corner. Make sure that the sponge is not overloaded. Apply the initial prints randomly and then fill in.

ERRORS

Beware of errors, such as blobs caused by not removing the excess on the card, or swirls from over-enthusiastic twirling of the sponge while it is still in contact with the surface.

If the error is made early on and has no neighbours, it can be wiped off with the relevant solvent. However, this is not often the case, and wiping can lead to smudging, which endangers the whole effect. If in doubt, blot the offending print with a tissue. When it is dry, fiddle through the base or ground colour using an artist's brush and short, staccato movements.

Sponging on a multicoloured ground

Sponging on a multicoloured ground is often used to introduce a direction of influence, rather as striped wallpaper gives a feeling of height, and bands of colour across a wall can give a sensation of width. This technique can be employed subtly to lift or widen a room.

Equipment

Brush or roller
Ground paint
Glaze or paint
Masking tape
Marine sponge
Paint tray
Card
Artist's brush
Painter's mate
Tissues

✳ Further information

Equipment *p.22*

1 Apply stripes or bands of colour to the surface with a brush or roller. Low-tack masking tape will help keep the borders neat. Allow to dry.

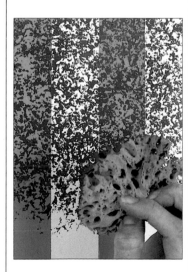

2 Using a dampened marine sponge charged with glaze, cover the surface with prints. The colour should link with one of those used for the background. Here, the dark blue is allied to the grey, and therefore "attacks" the white stripes.

3 The second colour to be sponged on is a pale blue. More closely allied to the white, it breaks up the grey stripes.

4 The finished effect, although similar to that of sponging on a plain ground, conveys an almost subliminal sense of direction which can enhance the proportions of a room.

Sponging onto a wet ground

The merging of two wet colours creates softer effects. Unlike other sponging, it is achieved by printing over a wet ground coat. This base is a mix of one part oil glaze to two parts oil-based undercoat or eggshell of the chosen colour, thinned by 10 per-cent with white spirit. It can be applied by brush or roller. If a large area, such as the wall of a room, is to be finished in this way, drying of the ground coat will need to be borne in mind. If possible, work with another person, one of you applying the ground coat from ceiling to floor in sections one metre (3 ft) wide, the other sponging on the glaze or top coat. The application of the base coat should be controlled to allow time for the sponging to be completed on each strip. The dual application, which is common when glaze is first applied and then manipulated, allows enough time for the complete novice to achieve a good-quality finish over a large surface.

1 Apply the ground coat, a mixture of one part glaze to two parts paint, thinned by 10 percent with white spirit or turpentine substitute.

2 Sponge on the glaze coat. The technique is the same as for sponging on a dry ground, but you will need to load the sponge with a greater amount of glaze.

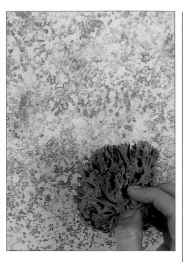

3 Fill in, remembering to use the sponge at different angles to achieve a non-repetitious effect.

Equipment

Ground paint or glaze mixture
Paintbrush or roller
Marine sponge
Paint or glaze
Paint tray

✱ Further information

Equipment *p.22*

4 The finished effect is a softer version of sponging on with a fossil-stone quality.

Sponging off

This is a subtracted effect*, normally achieved with oil, although water-based glazes can be used over small areas. The glaze is applied with a roller or brush in the usual way, and then lifted off with a dry synthetic sponge, leaving a subtle effect similar to that of stipple*. You will need a number of sponges to apply the finish to a large surface. Tear the sponges into manageable sizes, and use the rough surface to produce the effect. For a bolder result, wring the sponges out in white spirit before use – but only if you are using an oil glaze. The completed effect should be a fine undulating finish with subtle movement and depth.

Equipment
Paint or glaze
Brush or roller
Dry, synthetic sponge
White spirit

✱ Further information
Applied and subtracted finishes *p.15*
Stippling *p.104*
Applying Mediums *p.16*

1 Apply the glaze without too much attention to brush marks. No laying off* is necessary.

2 Place the rough face of the sponge onto the surface to remove the glaze. Sponge the area roughly, using a similar technique to sponging on.

3 To fill in, lift the darker areas of glaze which were missed in the initial sponging.

4 Sponging off results in a softer, more overall effect than sponging on.

Stipping

Standard fine
stipple

◆

Coarse stippling

◆

Multicoloured
stippling

◆

Blended or tonal
stippling

Originally stippling was a way of distributing paint or glaze as evenly as possible. Many original paint effects involved stippling the ground or glaze colour prior to finishing. Authentic standard stipple is only achievable with transparent oil glaze, because the effect is so fine that the medium must possess enough hold to preserve its texture without flowing back. The subtlety and finish of this effect are also enhanced by the glowing transparency of an oil glaze. The glaze is applied with a brush or roller and laid off in the usual way for subtracted finishes*. A brush is then bounced across the surface with a pouncing movement, producing a fine pepper-like orange-peel finish.

Stippling is not an effect to undertake lightly. The physical effort required is greater than with any other finish. You will have to bounce the brush over the entire surface, so the bigger the brush the better when decorating a room. For such sizeable areas, it may be advisable to purchase a large stippling brush*. These are extremely expensive, however, and it's worth experimenting with some alternatives beforehand. A lily bristle decorator's dusting brush*, a broom head, a soft-bristle hairbrush, a shoe brush – all have been used with success.

*Standard fine
stipple*

A standard stipple requires top-quality preparation*: the effect is so finely textured that any flaw stands out like a sore thumb. After applying the glaze, bounce the brush across the surface, letting the bristles act like springs. Hold the brush at right angles to the surface to prevent skidding. Angle the

attitude of the brush to ensure that any lines caused by the brush shape are not as obvious as they would be if they were horizontal or vertical. Rub the brush clean regularly with a rag to maintain a uniform effect.

When working on a large surface, and following the recommendations for subtractive finishes, it is advisable to step away from the area to check the overall look, and to jab the brush lightly at any dark patches. This effect needs extreme caution because of its fine texture. Any accidental damage will be very evident. If damage occurs and the surface is still wet, reapply glaze quickly to the affected area and restipple. If, however, the glaze has begun to dry, or tack off, a renewed application of

1 When finishing an edged surface, such as this table-top, apply the glaze first to the edge and then to the larger top.

glaze will react against the tacky glaze and worsen the fault. If you can live with the fault, leave it. If not, remove the glaze with rags and white spirit, and allow the surface to dry for at least two hours before reapplication.

Equipment

Brush or roller
Glaze
Stipple brush
Rags
Mutton cloth

✱ Further information

Applied and subtracted
finishes *p.15*
Brushes/Equipment *p.22*
Preparation *p.17*
Applying mediums *p.16*

3 Stipple the edge first, because this cannot be done without overlapping the top.

4 Stipple the top, holding the brush at right angles and allowing the bristles to act like springs. Remember to wipe the brush occasionally with a rag to remove the glaze.

5 Use a piece of mutton cloth* wrapped around your finger to achieve a wiped, dragged look over the moulding.

2 Lay off* the glaze lightly with an unloaded brush.

6 The finished piece demonstrates the subtlety of this technique.

3 Apply the ivory black in the same way, but to a much lesser extent. Take great care throughout to create an uncontrived finish.

5 Use the same technique to complete the softening, but this time in an east to west and west to east direction. Be sure to keep the brush clean at all times by wiping it with a lint-free rag.

4 Using a soft-haired brush and barely touching the surface, blend the colour into the varnish. Maintain the softening stroke at a constant angle until the whole surface has been treated. The brush should slant toward the direction in which it is moved, so as to lessen the force of the bristles on the surface. Soften the surface in both directions following the same line – for example, from north to south and south to north.

6 The finished panel is here being cleaned so that the edges may be gilded.

Quartered red tortoiseshell

This technique is a more elaborate version of the last, using a different colourway. Tortoiseshell was often inlaid in very thin veneers, which lend themselves to a quartered effect. The design is here made more effective by the choice of a bright red ground, which echoes the vermilion used long ago by harpsichord casemakers.

After applying the red pre-mixed paint, measure the surface to be finished and find its centre. You can complete the diagonally opposing quarters simul-taneously, but you must mask the remaining areas with clear adhesive tape, as masking tape will allow the varnish to bleed through. Dark oak varnish is again the medium, but only black is used in the figuring. When the effect is completed and dry, smooth it with wet-and-dry paper*, and finish it with two or three coats of varnish*.

Equipment

Red ground coat and application brush
Clear adhesive tape
Dark oak varnish and application brush
Ivory black, artists' oil colour
Artist's brush 0 or 00
Softening brush, such as a soft-haired cutter
Lint-free rag

* Further information

Sanding *p.21*
Varnishes *p.29*
Mediums *p.10*
Brushes *p.24*

2 Fiddle the black oil colour onto the wet surface with the artist's brush using short, staccato movements. The paint marks should generally lie in one diagonal.

3 Use a soft-haired brush – here a graining brush called a cutter* – to soften the colour in both directions along the diagonal already established. Keep the brush clean and dry by rubbing it on a lint-free rag.

1 Having masked the appropriate areas, with clear adhesive tape, apply the dark oak varnish.

4 Blend the effect further by changing the line of softening to one at 90° to your original diagonal.

Clean the brush, and finally soften in the original directions again.

Artistic effects

This section deals with special techniques that are not, strictly speaking, paint effects, but are nevertheless used decoratively on both walls and furniture. All the effects included in this section can be tackled by the amateur with a degree of success. This is particularly true of stencilling and découpage. However, if you want to progress to a high level of achievement, particularly with *trompe l'oeil*, you will need to have some artistic ability and be prepared to practice; the examples included in the gallery required a high degree of skill and training. The *trompe l'oeil* technique included here is designed to get you started and, perhaps, to inspire you to pursue it further. Gilding, on the other hand, although one of the more demanding techniques, requires no special skills and can transform picture frames, furniture, fire mantels and ornamental pillars.

Découpage

The technique of mounting and varnishing cut-out designs is thought to have developed in 17th century Italy alongside japanning (high gloss lacquering in the Japanese style), and in competition with Far-eastern imports of lacquered work. At first hand-coloured engravings were used, sealed with many coats of lacquer. The Victorians loved this effect and often went overboard with heavy finishes, especially on firescreens and trays.

An attractive découpage can be created with a minimum of technical skill. The art of this effect lies not so much in the selection, cutting out and sticking of the designs but in the way they are arranged on the surface and the choice and application of the finishing varnish. A period or rural look is appropriate, and it is important to avoid an over-symmetrical pattern. Material is not hard to find, and it is a good idea to amass a file of pictures that catch your eye from magazines, calendars, catalogues and old wrapping paper. There are even specialists who will supply printed designs intended for this effect. The inclusion of metal leaf can add an extra dimension to the composition. A photocopier can be a great help in reproducing, enlarging or reducing a design to fit an overall scheme. Test a spare patch of your chosen paper with a little varnish to check that it does not turn transparent and reveal print from its other side. You can use any painted suface as a base, providing it is spotlessly clean.

Map out your design on a sheet of paper the same size as the surface, and don't begin gluing until you are completely happy with the composition. Cut out the pieces using a scalpel and cutting board, and spray them on the print side with a fixative spray to ensure that the colours will not run when the varnish is applied. Use a PVA glue to stick the pieces onto the surface, making sure that they do not overlap. Meeting edges must be butt-jointed. Ensure that all edges are coated with glue and stuck down flat. A tiny artist's brush* can be used to apply glue to small pieces, and a little wallpaper roller will help to expel any air bubbles when flattening. Leave the piece to dry at room temperature before applying any coats of varnish. The varnish can be tinted* to give an impression of age or treated with a craquelure effect*.

Equipment

Pictures for mounting
Scissors
Scalpel
Cutting board
Colour fixative spray
PVA glue and application brush
Small wallpaper roller
Varnish and application brush

✱ Further information

Brushes *p.24*
Varnishing *p.29*
Craquelure *p.37*

1 Cut out a suitable printed design with a pair of scissors, and decide which parts of it to use. Where there is more than one element, you will need to plan your composition on a sheet of paper the same size as your surface.

2 Carry out further cutting with a scalpel and cutting board. When you are satisfied with your planned layout, spray the pieces on the print side with a fixative spray.

3 Apply PVA glue to the back of the pieces with an appropriately sized artist's brush, ensuring that all edges are coated.

4 Press the pieces carefully onto the surface, making sure that they are flat, especially around the edges. Any adjoining pieces need to be butt-jointed.

Gilding

Loose leaf gilding

◆

Transfer gilding

◆

Gilding with powder

Equipment

Gold size and application brush
Gold or metal leaf
Gilder's cushion
Gilder's knife
Gilder's tip
Gilder's whiting
Pounce bag
Cotton wool ball
Mop

Gilding has been used as a form of decoration for thousands of years throughout the world, from the jewellery of the Incas to the ancient Egyptians' lavish ornaments of death. And, perhaps even more astounding, the methods used have barely changed. Although some types of gilding require much skill and practice, the method described here should prove relatively easy.

The term gilding does not only refer to gold, but encompasses the application of all metal leaves and powders, from silver and platinum to bronze, aluminium and gold-coloured alloys.

The ancient process of gilding can be thought of as one of the earliest faux finishes because the intention was to convey the impression of solid gold in a less costly structure covered with only a thin skin of precious metal. The problem, therefore, is how to glue this fine sheet of gold or other metal to the surface, having previously ensured that the surface is exquisitely prepared, often with the use of gesso*.

Oil- and water-based

Traditionally there are two varieties of true gilding. As with many paint effects, these are water-based and oil-based. Water gilding is highly delicate and can be ruined by dampness. It is also a far more difficult technique than oil, involving only water with a minute addition of glue as an adhesive, and it cannot be used with transfer leaf.

Oil gilding – also known as mordant gilding – is therefore recommended here. Apart from being easier to undertake, it is much more adaptable and less vulnerable.

Gold size

The glue used in oil gilding is called gold size. This is a special mixture containing linseed oil, a drier such as lead oxide, and copal varnish. Turpentine is often added as a thinner to ease application. Sizes are often quoted in terms of their drying time: four-hour, eight-hour, or sixteen-hour size, for example. Drying time is important because the quicker the surface dries the less danger there is from dust or other pollution, but the slower it dries the more time you have to work and the better the gleam. "Quick japan size", which dries exceptionally fast – in one to two hours – is useful where the atmosphere cannot be controlled and dust particles may fall in the wet size, but it is correspondingly fragile and more prone to cracking.

As always, a balance must be found but above all it is essential to keep the atmosphere as clean as possible. Pieces which are small enough can be covered. Do not wear wool, and keep draughts to a minimum. Paint the size on evenly, or drying will be patchy and affect the adhesion of the leaf.

When gilding over gesso* it is wise to coat the ground with one or two coats of thinned shellac*. This seals the porous gesso and reduces the risk of a patchy gold size coat. If you use acrylic gesso*, you may not need a shellac coat.

Applying gold size

The area to be sized must dictate the shape and dimensions of the brush. Flat brushes are suitable for large areas and mouldings; round brushes are better for carvings and intricate details*. The brush should be of good quality, with long bristles to hold the size, yet firm enough to lay out the size evenly. Do not apply the size directly from the tin. It must be decanted into a clean paint kettle* or other container with a wire or thread tightly strung across the top. This strike wire will cause the size that is wiped clear of the brush to drain back into the container without forming bubbles. Only decant the amount of size needed for the job. More can be added if need be, but once the size has been decanted it should never be returned to the original tin, which is still clean and dust-free. Before any application, tack rag* the surface to remove any remaining dust.

When to gild

Once the size has been applied, the temptation to begin gilding is very great. However, if the gold or metal leaf is applied too early, it remains vulnerable to marks because the size underneath is still soft. What's more, the leaf will be dull and lifeless. The correct time to gild is when the size is practically dry. It is often suggested that you test this by drawing the back of your hand or finger gently over the surface to produce a squeak, and this can be useful, but if you try it too early, you may cause serious damage. Another sign used by some is that the size begins to lose its glossy texture when it is ready for gilding. However, the surest results come from testing trial patches of size, applying the leaves at timed intervals. That way, the weather conditions and the size mix, which are as important as the thickness of the size, can be involved, and a more accurate decision made.

The technique for applying transfer leaf is straightforward*, but if you want to use loose leaf, you will need a set of equipment* available from specialist suppliers, consisting of a gilder's cushion, knife and tip, and some gilder's whiting. A soft-haired brush known as a mop* is also useful for pressing the leaf into awkward areas, repairing faults and removing excess leaf.

✽ Further information

Gilder's equipment *p.28*
Preparation *p.17*
Gesso *p.20*
Mediums *p.10*
Brushes *p.24*
Equipment *p.22*
Making a pounce bag *p.28*

Loose leaf oil gilding

Before gilding, lightly dust your gilder's cushion, knife and tip with gilder's whiting (using a pounce bag*) to prevent the metal leaf from sticking. The leaves can be individually deposited onto the cushion as required, or en masse, whichever is more convenient to the

particular job. Cut the leaf with the gilder's knife, which should be kept in its loop underneath the cushion when not in use. The size of the leaf depends on the surface to be gilded, but you should allow a reasonable overlap. Hold the knife blade flat against the leaf, so that it maintains an even contact with the surface, and draw it once across the leaf to cut it. The next step is to flatten the leaf. Use the knife to pick up the leaf and turn it, and take time to play with the leaf on the cushion. Experiment with sliding the knife under the leaf and gently twisting it, while blowing delicately to remove wrinkles. There are no rules and no magical secrets. The object is simply

to smooth the leaf out in the best way you can.

When the cut leaves lie flat and unwrinkled on the cushion, prepare the tip to transfer them to the sized surface. Make sure your tip is smaller than the cut leaves, so that you will be able to position them accurately. Brush the tip over your cheek, so that it acquires enough oil from your skin to enable it to pick up the leaf. If this technique fails at first, rub a little moisturising cream on your cheek and try again. The leaf should be deposited onto the surface in one smooth action. If you make any movement when tip, leaf and size are together, the leaf will tear.

Continue applying the

1 Apply the gold size smoothly and evenly so that the whole area is ready for gilding at roughly the same time. Allow the size to tack off, having previously established its tacking time on a spare board.

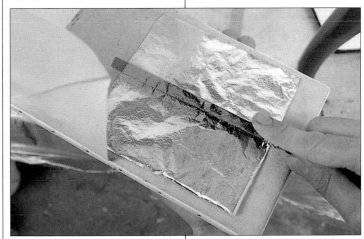

2 Cut the leaf to size using the gilder's knife on the cushion. Note how the knife blade is flat and the cut made with one pull. A sawing action would tear the leaf.

leaves in this way, each overlapping its neighbour by approximately 5 mm (³/₁₆ in). When you have applied six leaves press them against the surface with a cotton wool ball. Be careful to press the overlaps flat rather than lifting them upwards. Wrinkles will appear, but this is normal and will be rectified when the surface is brushed clean. Once the leaf has been pressed flat, begin gently brushing the excess loose leaf off the surface. These bits of leaf are called skewings and should be kept for future patching. As you progress across the area, odd faults will become apparent. Mending, or faulting, is achieved by pressing the skewings onto these areas. A mop or other soft-haired brush* can be employed to press down the gold and remove the excess leaf at the same time. However, this technique requires some practice.

5 Press the gold down with cotton wool or a lightly used mop.

3 Brush the gilder's tip over your cheek to pick up oil for adhesion and use it to lift the leaf from the cushion.

4 Apply the leaf to the sized ground in a gentle down-up movement. Any wavering at this point will cause the leaf to tear.

6 Brush the skewings off the surface, catching them in a pot or on the cushion for use in faulting or on later work. Carry out faulting by pressing the unused leaf onto any area missed by the initial gilding.

Transfer gilding

This technique was originally used by gilders when working outdoors, where loose leaf can be terribly difficult to control. The advantages of transfer leaf are obvious, in that manipulation can be undertaken by hand rather than by knife and tip. Transfer metal leaf can only be used in conjunction with gold size*. Apply the size coat in the same way as for loose leaf, and allow it to achieve its tack. If the leaf needs cutting, use long-bladed scissors or a scalpel and straight-edge. Cut the leaf with one snip or a single stroke of the scalpel to avoid tearing. Make sure that your working position gives support to your elbow or wrist to prevent undue movement as you apply the leaf to the sized surface. The transparent tissue backing will allow you to position it accurately. Place the leaf on the surface, and steady it with your spare hand as you stroke it into position with your fingers to ensure overall contact. Gently remove the backing to expose the newly gilded surface. The next leaf should overlap by approximately 5 mm (3/16 in). When you have completed the area, use the discarded tissues which still have leaf attached to carry out faulting*. Brush the surface clean with a mop* in the same way as with loose leaf.

Equipment

Gold size and application brush
Transfer gold or metal leaf
Mop
*Burnt umber antiquing glaze**
Rag

✳ Further information

Gold size *p.122*
Faulting *p.124*
Brushes *p.24*
Antiquing over gold *p.34*

2 Hold the transparent backing sheet with both hands and approach the surface with the leaf.

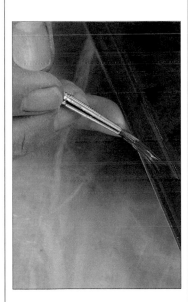

1 Apply the gold size using a suitable brush, and allow to tack off.

3 Steady your hands by leaning your elbow or wrist onto a support, and hold the leaf with one hand as you calmly smooth it into place with the other, taking care not to move it once it has made contact with the size. Remember to overlap each leaf by about 5mm (3/16 in).

4 Having pressed the leaf onto the surface with your fingers, carefully peel away the tissue backing.

5 When the application is complete, remove unwanted debris with a mop, and fault where necessary.

6 The gold can be complemented with the addition of antiquing glaze – in this case burnt umber.

Gilding with powder

Metal powders range from rich pale gold to dark bronze. Aluminium powder is also available. Their application is best achieved in a draught-free environment. When working with any fine-ground powders, it is advisable to wear a mask. This protects the lungs from contamination and lessens the possibility of breathing on, and therefore dispersing, the powder. Apply the gold size* in the same way as with loose leaf* or transfer leaf*, and allow it to tack off. Use a camel-hair or squirrel-hair mop* to

work the powder over the size and into any crevices. Allow the surface to dry for at least an hour before removing the excess powder with a soft cloth. Powder effects are liable to tarnish, so protect the surface with a coat of oil-based varnish.

Equipment
Gold size and application brush
Gold or bronze powder
Oil-based varnish and brush
Squirrel- or camel-hair mop
Soft duster or rag
Mask

✳ Further information
Gold size *p.122*
Gold fossil *p.92*
Loose leaf gilding *p.123*
Transfer gilding *p.125*
Brushes *p.24*
Varnishing *p.29*

1 Apply the gold size and allow it to become tacky.

2 Cover the sticky size with the dry powder, using the soft-haired mop to work it into all the details.

3 When the size has dried for at least an hour, gently remove the loose powder, using a soft duster or rag.

4 It is advisable to varnish gold or bronze powder, because it tends to tarnish.

GILDING WITH GOLD PAINT

This technique is often used to add details to a piece, such as a line or a small hand-painted design. The gold paint can be bought or you can mix your own using bronze or gold powder and either gold size* or a water-based glaze (as for gold fossil*). Whether your medium, is oil- or water-based, you will need to make a smooth, free-flowing but strong solution. If the mixture is weak, the gilding will be dull and lack definition. Apply it by brush.

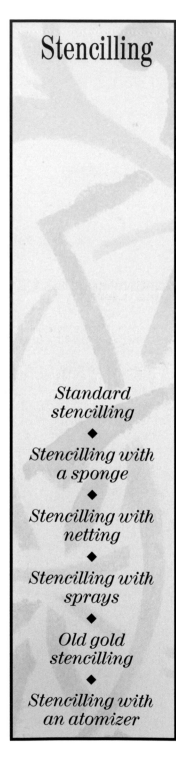

Stencilling

*Standard
stencilling*

◆

*Stencilling with
a sponge*

◆

*Stencilling with
netting*

◆

*Stencilling with
sprays*

◆

*Old gold
stencilling*

◆

*Stencilling with
an atomizer*

Stencils are known to have been used as far back as 3000 BC in China, where silks and paper were decorated. Since that time, many civilizations have employed this efficient decorative effect to enhance churches, tombs, floors, walls, textiles, furniture, books, trays and boxes. And no great artistic talent is required to achieve a very pleasing result. To some extent stencilling has suffered through its own success. The recent fashion for stencils has tended to pigeonhole the effect. The mere mention of a stencil can conjure up images of the folk-style birds, fruit and flowers which, although attractive, have recently been overplayed.

In fact, an enormously varied style can be achieved with stencils, from Chinese or Egyptian designs to the patterns of Tudor wall-hangings. Regency interiors were often edged with a design that was either stencilled or painted by hand. Stencils were popular in Victorian England, where they ranged from the austere to the frivolous. William Morris made extensive use of the method, as did many decorators of the Art Nouveau period. Charles Rennie Mackintosh included the technique in producing his unmistakable style. Louis Comfort Tiffany used stencilling in his famous commissions for the White House and Mark Twain's residence, thereby adding to the technique's standing in America.

Stencils can look ancient or modern, sharp or faded, and have the very useful ability to lend detail to an otherwise plain surface. Once a stencil has been cut, many different colours and textures can be used to vary the effect. Pre-cut stencils are readily available from art shops and DIY stores. If you want a quick and inexpensive effect, these can be a good, no-hassle choice. However, there is also much enjoyment to be had from cutting your own designs.

Choosing a design

First decide on the overall style of the piece or room. Often you can echo a motif from a fabric or plasterwork which will complement the scheme. Next, consider how you might reinforce or modify the physical aspects of your subject area. Do walls present too large an expanse that needs cutting into panels? Is the ceiling too high, and might the room benefit from a chair rail or dado? A picture rail frieze could expand the ceiling area, or perhaps the cornice needs strengthening. Try to see the room or piece as a whole with a clear idea of what you would like to achieve. Some rough sketches of your ideas may help. With an overall plan in mind, you can try out promising styles and sizes of stencil with paper cut-outs pinned or taped to your chosen surface. These could be cut to the pattern of a ready-made stencil, traced from an existing source, or be an entirely new design. You can enlarge or reduce the design with the aid of a photocopier or overhead projector.

A key factor in stencil design is the arrangement of ties. The ties are the parts of the stencil which have to remain in place to support the open internal areas. For example, the letter O would require ties to prevent the centre from falling out. The ties should be allowed for prior to tracing out the design, and should be wide and numerous enough to support the design with ease. When stencilling is complete, they can be touched in as desired.

Even a simple stencil should have little notches or pencilled marks, known as registration marks, to enable you to line up each successive print in a frieze or border. If you are combining two or three differently coloured stencils, the registration marks are even more critical to placing the stencils in the correct position. Registration marks are established, when the stencil is cut.

Equipment
Tracing paper
Stencil card
Cutting mat
Hard pencil
Stencil knife or craft knife

CUTTING A STENCIL

1 Trace out the design, leaving the ties in position.

2 Turn the completed tracing over onto the stencil card, and re-trace.

3 Place the card on the cutting mat, and use the stencil knife or craft knife to cut the stencil out, always working towards the body.

4 Registration marks should be made on the original tracings. This is especially important in the case of a double stencil, so that the design can be aligned on the surface.

5 Transfer the registration marks to the stencils by overlaying the tracings and remarking the points. Make these into a small hole or notch through which you can make a pencil mark to line up the cut stencils.

Standard stencilling

A standard stencil is normally applied with a stubby stencil brush* of the appropriate size, loaded with thick water- or oil-based colour. Test the print first on a spare piece of card. The drier the print, the less danger there is of seepage. Steady the stencil plate with low-tack masking tape to ensure a clean print.

Equipment
Stencil
Low-tack masking tape
Stencil brush
Thick oil- or water-based paint (two colours)
Card
Soft pencil

✳ Further information
Brushes *p.24*

1 Secure the stencil in position on the surface, with low-tack masking tape.

2 Load the brush with colour and check the print on some card or a spare area of stencil. Pounce the brush onto the perforated portions of the stencil, angling the brush to make sure all exposed areas are covered. Occasionally a bristle may creep under the stencil, but this merely adds to the charm of the effect.

Themes

A decorative paint effect can only be judged in its overall setting. The gallery of rooms, walls, furniture and objects assembled here, demonstrates a range of effects from the Techniques section. They are designed to show the techniques in a room setting or on specific objects and to inspire you to experiment. This gallery section is just a taster; if you keep your eyes open you will soon notice paint effects all around you in bars, restaurants, offices and people's homes. Often you won't realize that you are looking at a paint effect until you have actually touched the "marble" or "wood" and found that it is false.

Floors

Treating a floor with paint effects can transform the appearance of a room. Many effects are suitable, from combing* and marbling* to stencilling* and *trompe-l'oeil**, depending on the setting and the desired mood. When choosing your effect, consider the area as a whole and visualize the overall pattern of your planned design in relation to the shape of the room and the furniture it will contain.

As with most jobs, planning and preparation* are the key to success. The floor must be made good before any paint is applied. If you are working on floorboards, mend all loose and damaged boards, fixing them securely with nails or screws. Next, ensure a smooth and even surface by sanding* the entire floor with a belt sander. These can be hired from most hire shops. Then follow the sequence indicated for wood preparation*. Avoid sealing off the cracks between each board as these allow movement and air circulation, and stopping them could cause dampness.

✳ Further information

Surface preparation *p.19*
Sanding *p.21*
Combing *p.49*
Marbling *p.75*
Stencilling *p.128*
Trompe-l'oeil p.136

JASON BURKE/DAVID MENDAL
▲ This wonderful floor would require artistic ability to emulate. The peacock design was painted in oils onto stripped floorboards, sealed with matt varnish and polished with beeswax.

THOMAS LANE
▶ Although this beautiful floor looks as if it has been made in a mixture of natural woods, in fact the entire expanse has been painted with oils and then lacquered. Some of the design has been done freehand and some has been stencilled.

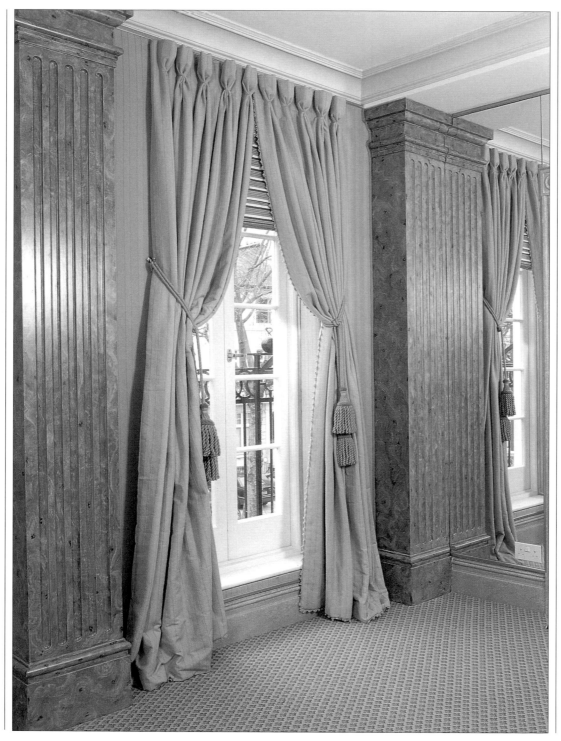

SIMON CAVELLE
◄ These twin fluted pilasters have been treated with a faux walnut grain which warms and enriches them and provides a frame for the French window. The colour carries through the line from the ceiling and is light enough to blend with the neutral shades of the room.

TANIA VARTAN
▼ *Trompe-l'oeil*, featuring a motif suitably evocative of sweet music, poetry and dreams, uses oil on canvas to create a wonderfully romantic headboard backed with blue sky.

PETER FARLOW
► This imposing room scheme eschews wallpaper for a stencil design which has been employed over a green wash. The colour is continued and deepened in the heavy, opulent marbling of the dado and the frame of the mahogany grained doors. The striking floor pattern is made of inlaid wood.

Doors

Doors are often overlooked when planning a decorating scheme. This is a pity since the door is a focus of attention as you enter a room – it heralds what is to come. The door, together with the supporting architrave, lends importance to the room, even before you see the room itself.

As a door is opened it will often glint in the light, revealing any flaws in the finish. This means it is particularly important to prepare* the door surface well (making sure it is sanded* until smooth) and to finish it with sealer or polish.

The handle should complement the finish or style of the door – a cheap modern handle, for example, will totally ruin an old panelled door, however beautifully it has been finished.

❋ Further information

Preparation *p.21*
Sanding *p.19*

RICHARD LOWSLEY WILLIAMS
▲ Burr walnut graining transforms this ordinary panelled door. Its air of grandeur is reinforced by the stone blocking treatment of the wall and the textured stone skirting.

RICHARD LOWSLEY
WILLIAMS
◀ The sober stability of faux
stone blocks is here
contrasted with the natural
strength of an undressed
stone effect. Techniques for
both are similar, but the
plaster for the rough-hewn
effect is worked over more
vigorously before painting to
achieve its coarser texture.

JASON BURKE/JONATHAN
BRUNSON
▲ Rich yellow walls
complement the mahogany
graining of an unusual piece
that doubles as dining room
cabinet and concealed door
to the kitchen. Achieving a
finish of this quality requires
skill and patience – eight
coats have been applied
ranging from an eggshell base
through flogging,
checkrolling, glazing,
varnishing and antiquing.

JASON BURKE/JONATHAN
BRUNSON
▶ This sumptuous entrance
to a woodgrained study
achieves its effect through the
contrast between simple off-
white and rich gold. The gold
is a mixture of bronze powder
and cellulose lacquer.

Fireplaces

RUPERT FORBES ADAM
▶ This delightfully patterned fire surround with its subtle shading is gently complemented by the pale green ragging of the walls.

BILL HOLGATE
▼ This classically inspired broken pediment design has been finely marbled over golden yellow to suggest a discreet opulence. This is a good example of how paint effects benefit from subtlety, particularly when the ground is unusual or dramatic.

▲ These seemingly different door effects were both achieved by dragging. The four-panel door has received a standard dragging treatment. The other door has been dragged with the aid of tape to produce mitre joints which match its construction.

If you are lucky enough to have a fireplace in your room, it makes a natural focal point. There may already be an existing mantel shelf and fireplace surround or you may want to create an entirely new one. In either case, your choice of finish will be dictated by the kind of atmosphere you want to convey. A marble surround, for example, will immediately suggest a formal decor, while a brick surround may lend itself to a country look.

Marbling*, graining* and *trompe l'oeil** will all create spectacular focal points which contrast with the decor, while softer effects such as sponging can tone in with the surrounding walls, meaning that attention is focused more on the decorative objects on the mantel, or on the picture above the fireplace.

❋ Further information
Marbling *p.75*
Graining *p.63*
Trompe l'oeil p.136

Furniture

Tables

◆

Chairs

◆

Cabinets

Furniture lends itself particularly well to paint effects. Traditional designs can be shown to their best using marbling* and graining* techniques. More contemporary pieces benefit from the fresh use of colour, which has never before been available in such a wide and exciting choice. As a rule, ornate furniture profits from subtle treatment, and a simple design can often be enhanced by a bold finish. Colour can modify the character and even the apparent dimensions of a piece. Just as dark clothes may have a slimming effect, so a dark colour tends to reduce the thickness of the legs on a table or chair. Bright, sunny colours give a country-cottage look, and dark, rich shades convey an air of elegance and refinement.

Painted furniture demands a much higher quality of finish than that of walls, and it can be more intricate to work on. It helps to turn a table or chair upside down and treat the innermost surfaces first. Often it is advisable to allow one area to dry before continuing, and you may occasionally need to varnish areas that could be spoiled if left unprotected. All furniture should be safeguarded from wear and tear by two or three coats of varnish at least.

✻ Further information

Marbling *p. 75*
Graining *p. 63*
Varnishing *p. 29*

Tables

The word table derives from the old French *tablel* meaning a *tableau* or painted scene. Ironically, tables today are seldom given an interesting paint finish. Instead, they are simply stained, varnished or glossed. Decorative paint effects allow you the opportunity to try something different – marbling, woodgraining, lapis lazuli, malachite, spattering, dragging, pickling, liming, *trompe l'oeil* – these are just some of the ways of turning an ordinary table into an exciting decorative accessory.

Obviously, tables differ dramatically in build and appearance – ranging from a robust kitchen table with scrubbed top and heavy legs to a delicate occasional table with such fine legs that the top seems to float. When considering the decoration of a table, ask yourself how it will be used and spend some time considering its design. The finish should complement the piece of furniture, not fight it.

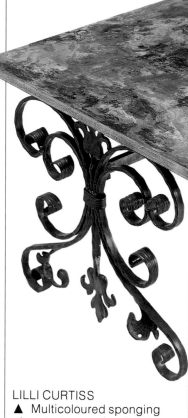

LILLI CURTISS
▲ Multicoloured sponging gives texture and weight to this modern coffee table. The stone effect suits the wrought iron design, and the choice of colour prevents it from appearing too heavy.

JAN CAVELLE
▲ The subtlety of a grey over white rag roll creates a balanced look for this Regency-style table.

THOMAS LANE
◀ This oak table has been stripped and then limed. All areas to be painted were masked during the liming process. The table edges and central design were painted with oils.

ROGER F. SEAMARK
▶ The antiqued glazes on this table pick up the blue in chairs and walls to contribute to the romantic pastoral theme of this room with its air of chic prettiness.

THE BERMUDA COLLECTION
▼ This understated table, antiqued with a lovely honey-coloured craquelure holds a surprise in its two *trompe-l'oeil* postcards.

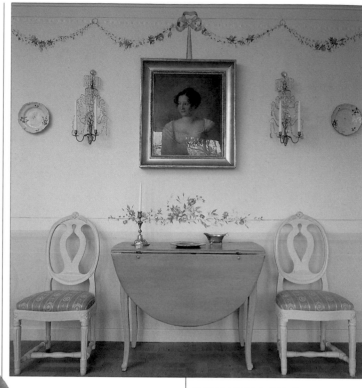

DERWENT UPHOLSTERY LIMITED
▶ Red over grey dragging gives these tables an oriental feel, which has been emphasized by the choice of curtain material and ornaments. Entirely different effects can be produced by varying the colours.

◀ A chess table decorated with découpage in the rococo style. The gold designs evoke the noble and ancient origins of the game, and the craquelure varnish adds to the feeling of antiquity.

LILLI CURTISS
▲ The charming proportions and details of this dainty table have been highlighted with antiqued gold leaf. Notice where the red ground has been allowed to show here and there through the gold.

Cabinets

Kitchen cabinets or units, more than any other item of furniture, require protective finishing. Regardless of the paint effect you choose, always finish with several coats of polyurethane varnish. Kitchen units are a popular subject for decorative paint effects and a successful finish can make all the difference to the appearance of the kitchen. Liming, pickling, dragging, distressing, colour wash and stencilling are just some of the choices available.

An ordinary non-kitchen cabinet receives less wear and tear, but you still need to think about the demands that will be made upon it and to consider the design. Does it have drawers, doors, or both? How are these fitted to the carcase? Do the drawer fronts stand proud or lie flush with the frame? All these moving parts need to be checked before you start decorating. Before you begin painting, make sure that all moving parts are masked to prevent a build-up of paint that will jam or impede their movements. Never paint the drawer runners (pieces of wood that the drawer slides on), as this will impede their smooth operation.

THOMAS MASARYK
▲ The harmonious finish for this Oriental piece is provided by distressing with different shades of oil glaze used over wood.

GONZALO GOROSTIAGA
◀ *Trompe-l'oeil* gives the impression of an untidy cupboard, with a romantic collection of contents. The piece has been distressed, which contributes to its country feel.

PAVILION ORIGINALS LIMITED
▶ This stencilled cabinet, blends with the dragged stripes of the wall, creating a fresh relaxed atmosphere due to its colours and graceful symmetrical patterning. The lines that partially frame the design anchor it to its setting. Without them the design would lack focus.

THOMAS MASARYK
▼ The diversity of colouring and effects achievable in marbling is displayed by this desk. The inset geometrical design is reminiscent of illuminated manuscripts.

MARK WILKINSON
▲ This Provençal style dresser has been painted with layers of blue-green colour wash, antiqued by rubbing, and waxed to achieve a translucent effect.

JOYCE HOWARD
► This detail from a dresser shows what can be achieved with some artistic skill. The design is drawn on tracing paper, transferred, painted, antiqued and then varnished.

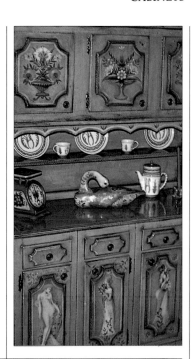

JASON BURKE/JONATHAN BRUNSON
▼ A mixture of burr walnut and fantasy woodgraining provides a fitting setting for the leatherbound books in this study. Oil glazes were applied over a water-based ground and then finished with varnishes – five coats in total.

PAVILION ORIGINALS
LIMITED
▲ Surfaces dragged in clear pale lemon glaze make this Scandinavian style kitchen appear more spacious. Unadorned, it could be bland or over-cool. But the strawberry stencils provide the simple note that gives the room its charm.

SMALLBONE
▶ The paintwork in this kitchen has been distressed to imitate the effect of wear and tear, giving the warm, relaxed atmosphere of a much used and loved room.

SIMON CAVELLE
► This new alcove cupboard has been treated with a pale antiquing effect, given definition by the gilded mouldings, and topped with a highly polished faux slate effect which picks up the dark marble from the fireplace.

MARK WILKINSON
▼ Light sponging in a warm salmon pink gives this kitchen an atmosphere at once elegant and intimate.

MARK WILKINSON
► This classy kitchen with its twisted columns and uncluttered cornice is skilfully stained to add weight and importance to various sections and to bring out the knots and grain of the wood. The walls are treated with the gently blurred wash effect known as scumbling.

SMALLBONE
▲ Pretty soft-toned stencil designs over dragged blue are given definition by the strong box lines. The stencil pattern has been varied to suit the dimensions of the doors and drawers.

Decorated accessories

Almost any item for the home can be given a decorative paint treatment. Mirror and picture frames, chests, wastepaper bins, boxes, clocks – the list is endless. Cheap items, picked up in secondhand shops and sales, can be entirely transformed with clever use of découpage*, stencilling*, *trompe l'oeil** and other paint effects.

Smaller items, particularly when you are new to paint effects, are less daunting than major projects such as an entire room or a large piece of furniture. You can feel free to experiment and to learn and, as a result, you can have a great deal of fun for a minimum amount of expenditure.

The pictures in this section show a small sample of decorative accessories, ranging from chests to milk churns, with the aim of sparking off your creativity.

* Further information

Découpage *p.120*
Stencilling *p.128*
Trompe l'oeil p.136

CAMILLA J. H. REDFERN
▼ These two imposing torchères, or candle-holders, have been painted black and skilfully gilded to give the brilliant but mellow finish appropriate to an antique object.

GONZALO GOROSTIAGA/
THE BERMUDA
COLLECTION/THE STENCIL
LIBRARY/JOYCE HOWARD
◀▼▶ Four different
treatments for old chests
illustrate the diversity of styles
achievable with paint.
Trompe-l'oeil gives an illusory
peep at a mellowed and non-
existent collection of sports
equipment; highly varnished
stencilling in vibrant colours
on black conjures up the folk
art of the canal narrow boats;
a blanket box has been
colour-washed and stencilled
in muted colours, then rubbed
to emphasize its age; and
hand painted figurative
designs have been given an
antiqued finish.

JANE DARBY DESIGNS
▲ A hat box delicately decorated with découpage and antiqued with a golden varnish reflects the fanciful details of a bygone age of elegance.

CHARLOTTE OAKES
▶ This arabesque wall sconce is the ideal ground for a verdigris effect, which lends it the characteristic blue-green patina of weather-worn antique metalwork.

► This oak clock has been stripped and then limed. Oak is particularly suitable for liming because of its open grain.

ANGELA SHAW
▼ This découpage in luscious colours softened by a pale green ground has been antiqued with a craquelure varnish to give it a rich but rural look reminiscent of past times.

JANE DARBY DESIGNS
▲ A bold découpage in light-filled colours, given depth by the rounded surface and dark ground, assigns this old milk can a new role as a beautiful decorative object.

CHRISTIAN THEE

◄ This screen, designed to stand in front of a window, adds humour to its jungle view with the inclusion of monkeys peeping through the greenery. The scene, which hints at the exotic imaginary landscapes of Rousseau, is given increased perspective by the box, which has been treated with the same effect.

GONZALO GOROSTIAGA

◄ A wooden screen painted in a *trompe-l'oeil* manner. Clever use of light and shade in the fabric folds, and colouring that echoes and enriches that of the background, draws the eye to admire the effect itself rather than simply seeking to deceive it.

MARK WILKINSON

▼ This screen has been heavily distressed to give the impression of a worn, battered piece of Provençal-style furniture.

CAMILLA J. H. REDFERN
▼ This ornate mirror frame has been gilded and gently antiqued using a raw umber glaze. The patina of age gives the piece greater weight and style and will add elegance to any room.

ANGELA SHAW
◀ This pretty mirror frame, decorated with blue and gold mouldings and hand-painted floral designs, has been treated with craquelure to give it a faded, time-worn look. The fine cracks have been highlighted by rubbing in an umber glaze, without which they would be almost invisible.

JOYCE HOWARD
◀ This colourful folk art Father Christmas will brighten your festive season. Made from wood, it has been painted, antiqued and then varnished.

RUPERT HANBURY DESIGNS

▼ These wastepaper bins have been transformed by dragging and sponging. The dark lines gently emphasize their shapes and add interest.

LILLI CURTISS
▲ Silver leaf and gilding combine to make an elegant surround for a mirror. In this case, the mirror has an unconventional finish, making it more artistic than functional.

Index

NOTE Page references in **bold type** denote main sections concerning the subject indicated; page references in *italic type* indicate illustrations.

A

abrasive papers 21
accessories, decorated **165–71**
acrylic colours 10–11
acrylic lacquers 10–11
aerosol cans 131
aerosol varnish 30
Air Blaster 134–5
aluminium leaf 28
aluminium powder 126–7
antiquing **34–45**
   accessories *147*
   candle-holders *165*
   chair *157*
   chests *166*
   colour wash 36
   colours for 34
   cupboard *163*
   découpage 37–8
   hat box *167*
   mirror frames *170*
   rubbing 43, *157, 160, 166, 171*
   tables *154, 155*
aqua blue 133–4
Art Nouveau 128
Artex stippler 106
artists' acrylic colours 10–11
artists' brushes 23
artists' oil colours 10–11, 14
artists' powder paint 10–11
Arts and Crafts movement 84
atomizers 131, 134–5

B

badger-hair softeners 23–4, 25, 64, 65, 67
bagging 90
bamboo, faux **57–8**
basketwork combing 49–50
bathrooms *145, 147*
bird's-eye maple graining 33, 63, 64
black and gold marble 78–80
blanket box *166*
blues 13–14
   aqua 133–4
   lapis lazuli 33, **69–70**
   ultramarine 69
bronze powders 28, 69, 70, 126–7, 133–4, *147, 150*
browns 14
brushes **23–6**
   care and cleaning 26
   for dragging 54
   for spattering 96
   for stippling 104
   using 16
Buhl 111
burr walnut graining *143, 145, 149, 161*

C

cabinets 41, **158–64**, *158, 160*
candle-holders *165*
ceilings 9, *147*
cellulose lacquer 30
chairs 156–7, *156, 157*
check rolling **46**
chess table *155*
chests *166*
china 57, 128
Christmas figure *171*
clair bois 63–4
clear adhesive tape 22
clock *168*
coarse stippling 33

colour wash **147**
   antiquing 36
colour washing **47–8**
   walls 47
   wood 36, 47–8
colours **8–9**
   charts 14
   mixing 13–14
combing **49–53**
combs 26, 27, 49
concrete floors 18
corners, sponging 100
cornice, antiquing 42
cotton rags 22, 23
craquelure 37–9, *154, 155, 168, 171*
curling stencil 135
curtaining 54

D

deal furniture 84
découpage 37, 119, **120–1**, *155, 167, 168*
distemper 47
distressing 34, 75, 139, *156, 158, 162, 169*
   rubbed antiquing 43, *157, 160, 166, 171*
doors 16, *145, 148, 149, 150, 151*
draggers 24, 54
dragging **54–6**, 145, *151, 154, 162, 171*
   antiquing 40, 42
dressers *160, 161*
dust masks 22, 23
dust sheets 22, 23
dusting brushes 24

E

earthenware 18
eggshell 10–11, 13, *147*
Egypt, ancient 63, 75
Egyptian green marble 81–3
emulsion brush 25
emulsion glaze 10–11, 12, 92
emulsion paint 10–11, 16
emulsion wash 12
equipment **22–8**

F

Father Christmas *171*
faux bamboo 57–8
faux finishes 148
   bamboo **57–8**
   mahogany 63, 66–7, 148, 150
   porphyry 86–7
   stone 159
   tortoiseshell 111–15
   see also gilding; graining; marbling; trompe l'oeil
faux slate *163*
faux stone blocks 59–61
feathers 26
fiddling 113
Fiji 131
filberts 23, 26
finishes 15
finishing **29–31**
Fire of London 63
fireplaces *151*
fitches 24, 26
fleck spatter, antiquing 45
floggers 24, 54, 62
flogging **62**, *146*
floor cloths 142
floors **140–2**, *148*
   concrete 18
folk art *156, 166, 171*
Fowler, John 54
frames 63, 64, *170, 171*
French Revolution 64

frosting 88, 91
furniture **152–64**
fittings, antiquing 34, 41

G

garnetpaper 21
gesso 20
   gilding over 122
giant ruler 54
gilding 28, 119, **122–7**, *147, 170, 171*
   antiquing 34–5
   equipment 123
   loose-leaf foil 123–4
   oil- and water-based 122
   with paint 127
   with powder 126–7
   transfer 125–6
glass 18
glasspaper 21
glazes 10–11, **12–15**
   antiquing 34–5, *154*
   dragging 54–5
   safety 13
   yellowing 13
gloss 10–11, 16
gloss emulsion 10–11, 16
gloss varnish 29
goggles 22, 23
gold *150*
   in lapis lazuli 69
gold fossil 92–3
gold leaf 28, 122–3, 124, *155*
gold paint, in gilding 127
gold powder 69, 126–7
gold size 122–3, 124–6
   Japan varnish 10–11
gold stencilling 38–9
   off-spray 132–3
   old gold 133–4
gouache colours 10–11
graining 62, **63–8**, *148, 149, 150, 161*
   bird's eye maple 33, 63, 64
   mahogany 63, 66–7, *144, 148, 150*
   walnut *143, 145, 148, 149, 161*

graining rollers 26, 27, 68
greens 14
   malachite 73–4
   verdigris **116–17**, 167

H

hallways *144, 145*
Hamburg school 111
handles, antiquing 34, 41
hat box *167*
hawk 28, 60
headboard *148*
hog-hair softener 24

J

Japan gold-size varnish 10–11
japanning 120, 133
Jones, Inigo 59

K

kettle, paint 22, 23, 122
kitchens *146, 158, 162, 163, 164*

L

lacquers 10–11, 30, *140, 147*
lapis lazuli 33, **69–70**
laying off 16
laying-on trowel 28, 60

M

Mackintosh, Charles Rennie 128
mahogany effect 63, 66–7, *144, 148, 150*
malachite **73–4**
marble
   finishing 81
   softening 83
   veining 82–3
marbling 59, **75–83**, 139, *144, 147, 151, 160*
marblizing 75
masking tape 22
matt emulsion 10–11, 16
matt varnish 29
mediums **10–11**
metal leaf 122–3, 124
metal powders *see* aluminium; bronze; gold; silver
metal surfaces 19
milk churn *168*
mirror frames 63, 64, *170, 171*
   moiré effect 52–3
mops 24, 25, 123
Morris, William 128
mottlers 24, 25
mould 18
mutton cloth 22, 23, 92

lichen **94–5**
light and shade 136–7
liming **71–2**, 139, *153, 157, 168*
lining paper 18
London
   Fire of 63
   interiors 59
loose leaf oil gilding 123

N

newel post *143*
nitro-cellulose spray 10–11
Nottingham Castle 66

O

oak 63, *153, 168*
off-spray 132
oil, cleaning brushes after
    using 26
oil colours, artists' 10–11
oil glaze, transparent 10–11,
    63–4
oil varnishes 10–11, 29, 31
oil-based glazes 10, 12, 13
    in gilding 34–5
    graining 63–4
    yellowing 11, 13, 14
oil-based primer 10–11
old gold stencilling 133–4

P

paint, antiquing 39
paint kettle 22, 23
paint trays 26, 27
painter's mate 22
paints **10–17**
    applying 16
    types 10–11, 16
pale wood graining 63–4
palette knives 22
panelling 63, 64
parquet flooring *142*
pickling **84–5**
pilasters *148*
pine 63, 84
plaster 150
    applying 60
    finishing 59

mixing 59
    painting 17
    removing 17–18
    texturing 60–1
plastering 59–60
    tools for 28
plumb-line 22, 23
polishing 31
polyurethane varnish
    10–11, 29
porphyry **86–7**
pottery 18
pounce bag 28
powder paint, artists' 10–11
preparation **17–21**
primer 10–11
Provençal style *160, 169*
PVA 12, 30

Q

Queen's Chapel, London 59
Queen's House, Greenwich
    59
quick japan size 122

R

radiator brushes 23, 25
rag rolling 88–9, *153*
ragging 42, **88–93**, *146, 147,*
    151
ragging on 90–1
reds 14
Regency
    interiors 128
    style 153
registration marks 128, 129
rocker combs 26, 27
rococo style *155*
roller graining 33
rollers
    graining 26, 27, 68
    paint 16, 19

room dimensions 9
rubbed antiquing 43, *157,*
    160, 166, 171
rubber combs 26, 27, 51
ruler, giant 54
rust 19

S

safety 4, 13, 88
sanding 17–18, 21
sandstone **94–5**
Santa Fe style *146*
satin emulsion 10–11
satin varnish 29
scalpel 22
Scandinavian style *162*
schlag leaf 28
sconce *167*
scraper 18
screens *169*
scumbling 12, 94, *157, 164*
sealers 29–30
shades 9
shellac 10–11, 19
ships, repair of 66
Siena marble 33, 75–8
silicon carbide 21
silk emulsion 10–11
silver fossil 92, 93
silver leaf 28, *171*
sizes 122
slate effect *163*
spalters 24
spattering **96–7**, *145*
spirit level 22
sponges 26, 27
sponging 94, **98–103**,
    163–171
    on multicoloured ground
        101, *152*
    on wet ground 102
spot board 28
sprays 30, 132–3
    spray mist 132–3
stainers 10–11
staining 34, *164*
stairs *144*

room dimensions 9
standard decorators'
    brushes 23, 25
steel tapemeasure 22
stencil brushes 24, 25
stencilling 119, **128–35**, *140,*
    147, 148, 158, 162, 164,
    166
    with an atomizer 134–5
    curling stencil 135
    with netting 131–2
    old gold 133–4
    with a sponge 130–1
    with sprays 132–3
    standard 129–30
    walls *143, 147, 148*
stipple, antiquing 44–5
stippling **104–8**
    blended 108
    coarse 106
    multicoloured 107
    standard fine stipple 104–5
stippling brushes 24
stone blocking *144, 145, 149,*
    150
stone blocks, faux 59–61
stone effect 31, *152*
strike wire 30–1, 122
strippers 20
stripping 84
stucco 59
sugi **109–10**
sword brushes 24, 25

T

tables 152–5, *153, 154, 155*
    antiquing 44
tack rags 22
tapemeasure 22
tick rolling 46
Tiffany, Louis Comfort 128
tints 9
torchères *165*
tortoiseshell **111–15**
    blonde 114–15
    brown 111–12
    quartered red 113–14
tracing paper 22, 23
transfer gilding 123, 125–6

transparent oil glaze 10–11, 63–4
trompe l'oeil 119, **136–7**
  cabinet 158
  chest 166
  headboard 148
  screens 169
  table 154
  walls 144, 146
trowel 28, 60
Twain, Mark 128

U

ultramarine 69
undercoat 9, 10–11, 16
universal stainers 10–11

V

varnishes **10–11**, 29–30
varnishing 29–31
veining marble 82–3
verdigris **116–17**, 167
Versailles 111

W

Wall sconce 167
wallpaper, painting over 18
walls **143–51**
  colour washing 47
  dragging 54–5
  faux stone 59–60
  glazed 12
  painted 9, 145
  rag rolling 88–9
  stencilled 143, 147, 148
  trompe l'oeil 144, 146

walnut graining 143, 145, 148, 149, 161
wash 12
  see also colour wash; colour washing
wastepaper bins 171
water-based paints 16
  brush cleaning 26
water-based varnishes 29–30
water-staining 45
watered silk effect 51–2
wax
  finishing 31, 160
  painting preparation 19–20
weave effect 50–1
wet-and-dry paper 18, 21
White House, US 128
whiting 28
windows 16
wire brushes 19, 43
wire wool 20, 31, 34, 35
wood
  antiquing 36
  colour wash 47–8
  gesso 20
  liming 71–2
  painting preparation 19
  sugi **109–10**
  woodwork, dragging 56

Y

yellowing, oil-based glaze 11, 13, 14
yellows 14

Credits

The author would like to thank Sally MacEachern, Penny Cobb and Mary Senechal for their incredibly hard work and whole hearted support, Jo Foster for transcribing the manuscript, John Wyland for the step-by-step photography, and the entire staff of K.L.C. School of Interior Design for their enthusiastic help. A special thanks to Jenny Gibbs, Kate Young and my family, without whom this book would not have been possible.

Quarto would like to thank the following suppliers who loaned materials for photography or contributed materials for use in the demonstrations:

Airtoys, Unit 25, The Industrial Estate, South Dole, West Sussex;
Belinda Ballentine School of Painted Furniture, The Abbey Brewery, Malmesbury, Wiltshire, SH16 9AS;
J W Bollom & Co Ltd, P.O. Box 78, Beckenham, Kent BR3 4B;
C Brewer and Sons Ltd, 31 Capital Way, Capital Industrial Estate, Colindale, London NW9;
Andrew Farmer, **E Polton (Sundries Ltd)**, 273 Archway Road, London N6 5AA;
The Cast Iron Shop, 394 Caledonian Road, London N1 1DW;

Daler-Rowney, Daler-Rowney House, Bracknell, Berkshire, RG12 8ST/Daler Rowney USA, 1085 Cranbury South River Road, New Jersey 08831;
Finer Frames Ltd, 28 Tewkesbury Garden, London NW9;
John Myland Ltd, 80 Norwood High Street, London SE27 9NW;
Oakleaf Reproductions Ltd, Ling Bob, Main Street, Wilsden, Bradford BD15 0JP;
J H Ratcliffe & Co (Paints) Ltd, 135A Linaker Street, Southport PR8 5DF;
Sainsbury's Homebase.

Quarto would like also to thank the following for contributing pictures of their work and for permission to reproduce copyright material:

Rupert Forbes Adam, Richardson's, Skipworth, Selby, North Yorkshire, YO8 7SQ;
Belinda Ballentine School of Painted Furniture, The Abbey Brewery, Malmesbury, Wiltshire, SH16 9AS;
The Bermuda Collection, Jamie and Betsy Sapsford, Unit 63, Smithbrook Kilns, Cranleigh, Surrey GU6 8JJ;
Michelle Blackler, Studio Southwest, 49 Fulham High Street, London SW6;
Jason Burke/Jonathan Brunson, Alternative Interiors, 13 School Road, Hampton Hill, Middlesex TW12 1Ql;

Jan Cavelle, 7 Station Road, Clare, Suffolk CO10 8NJ;
Lilli Curtiss, 401½ Workshops, 401½ Wandsworth Road, London SW8 2JP;
Jane Darby Designs, Jopes Mill, Trebrownbridge Nr Liskeard, Cornwall PL14 3PX;
Sarah Delafield Cook, 7A Anhalt Road, London SW11 4N3;
Derwent Upholstery Ltd, Greenhill Industrial Estate, Greenhill Lane, Riddings, Derbyshire DE55 4BR;
John and Sheila Elliot, Elliot Studio Galleries, 304 Highmount Terrace, Upper Nyack-on-Hudson, New York 10960;
Peter Farlow, 199 Westbourne Grove, London W11 2SB;
Helen Fitzgerald, The Lane, Newark, East Sussex BN8 4QX;
Gonzalo Gorostiaga, 6 Puma Court, London, E1 6QG;
Susie Gradwell, Southview, Moorlynch, Bridgewater, Somerset TA7 9BU;
Rupert Hanbury, The Kernals, Bartlow, Cambridge;
Bill Holgate, The Bungalow, 62 Littlemoor Road, Clitheroe, Lancashire BB7 1EW;
Thomas Lane, Painted Interiors, 57 Wellington Row, London E2 7BB;
Richard Lowsley Williams, Flat 4, 82 Cambridge Gardens, London W10 6HS;
Thomas Masaryk, 4260 Main Street, Stratford, Connecticut, 06497, USA;
Charlotte Oakes, 376 St Johns Street, London EC1V 4NN;

Pavilion Originals Ltd, 6A Howe Street, Edinburgh EH3 6TD;
Camilla J H Redfern, 32 Abbey Business Centre, Ingate Place, London SW8 3NS;
Roger F Seamark, Karlavagen 68, 114 59 Stockholm, Sweden;
Angela Shaw, Flexford House, Hog's Back GU3 2JP;
Smallbone, 105–109 Fulham Road, London SW3;
The Stencil Library, Nesbit Hill Head, Stamfordham, Northumberland NE18 0LG;
Christian Thee, 49 Old Stage Coach Road, Weston, CT 06883, USA;
Tania Vartan, Ecole Et Atelier, Le Bariel, Rond Point Ste Claire, 06570, St Paul De Vence, France;
Sasha Waddell, c/o Codrington Furniture, Arch 80, Chelsea Bridge Business Centre, Queenstown Road, London SW8;
Mark Wilkinson Furniture, Overton House, Bromham, Wiltshire SN15 2HA.

Additional picture credits:

p12 **Peter Farlow** p13 **Simon Cavelle** p118–19 from top left **G. Gorostiaga, Susie Gradwell, Camilla J. H. Redfern** p138–9 from top left **Thomas Lane, Mark Wilkinson, Thomas Masaryk, Thomas Lane.**

Quarto would like to thank the following:

Theo Woodham Smith Public Relations for supplying transparancies of Mark Wilkinson's work; Halston PR Ltd for supplying work by Smallbone; The Royal Pavilion, Brighton; John Elliot for supplying transparancies of Joyce Howard's work.